Malibu
Beach
Recovery
Diet
Cookbook

Quick and Tasty Recipes to Help Break the Cycle of Alcoholism and Addiction

Malibu Beach Recovery Diet
Cookbook

Joan Borsten

and the Chefs of the Malibu Beach Recovery Center

 Vidov Publishing, Malibu

For information, contact:
Vidov Publishing
23823 Malibu Road
Malibu, CA 90265
Email: **info@vidovpublishing.com**
www.malibubeachrecoverydietcookbook.com

For foreign and translation rights, contact: **Nigel J. Yorwerth**
Email: **nigel@PublishingCoaches.com**

ISBN: 978-1-4951-2669-7

10 9 8 7 6 5 4 3 2 1

The text type was set in **Minion Pro**

This book is not intended to replace medical advice or substitute for treatment of substance abuse. If you are sick or suspect you are sick, you should see a physician. If you are taking prescription medications, abusing illegal drugs or alcohol or suffering from depression or anxiety, you should consult a medical professional about appropriate diet and treatment, as any change in diet can affect your medical condition. Certain foods can have adverse effects when combined with prescription drugs. Although this book is about food and diet, the authors and the publisher disclaim responsibility for any adverse effects arising from use of this diet. Finally, all references to dopamine and serotonin and their effects reflect current thinking in the neuroscientific community and vary according to individuals and their own body chemistry, including their genetics.

CONTENTS

Malibu Beach Recovery Diet Cookbook
Get Sober — Stay Sober

In "recovery speak," that special vocabulary used by people in the addiction industry, I am what is known as a "normie" — someone who, unlike the other 95 percent who work in this field, never had a problem with alcohol, street drugs or prescription pills. Initially, being a "normie" presented a big learning curve. Like many of the friends and families of the clients we treated, it was hard for me to accept the fact that addiction can become a chronic brain disease.

Most of our clients, I was told, would have low dopamine levels — dopamine being the brain's "happiness" neurotransmitter. They self-medicated to feel good. Some might have been born genetically predisposed to addiction, while others had depleted their dopamine levels through excessive drug and alcohol use and "addict behavior" such as living on fast food and coffee, running until they dropped and self-medicating for the "feel good" rush. Many could also suffer from depression, anxiety and panic attacks.

I knew that people diagnosed with diabetes, high cholesterol or high blood pressure can lower their "numbers" by changing the way they eat. According to what we have learned from neuroscience, healthy eating can also help put addiction into remission. That is why we made the decision to provide our clients with a low-glycemic diet.

I did some industrial espionage before we opened the center that revealed that few if any in the addiction industry seemed to care about the link between food and addiction to drugs and alcohol. I wrangled lunch invitations at several treatment centers and what I discovered was that whether the food was made by a former celebrity chef or by the clients themselves, it was laden with carbohydrates and sugar. It was then, and still is now, an addiction industry axiom that entering rehab means gaining 30 pounds.

The Malibu Beach Recovery Diet is based on the research of Michel Montignac, an executive in the French pharmaceutical industry who in 1986 created a revolutionary weight-loss diet for himself based not on counting calories but on classifying carbohydrates using a Glycemic Index. The principles he developed are now widely accepted. It is not by chance that most foods associated with dopamine production and regulation are also low glycemic. In many cases, dopamine levels can be enhanced by healthy eating rather than using drugs, alcohol or prescription mood stabilizers.

While we trained therapists, counselors and yoga teachers and renovated the house that would become the Malibu Beach Recovery Center, my friend Licia Jaccard, a graduate of Le Cordon Bleu Culinary School in Paris and a co-author of this cookbook, was translating Montignac's books from French.

The Montignac diet gave our chefs the opportunity to express themselves creatively and prepare fresh, seasonal food that was both delicious and beautiful to behold. The main ingredients they had to work with were fresh fruits and vegetables, whole grains, legumes, fish, poultry, beef, lamb, dairy products, oils, nuts and dark chocolate. The off-limit, high glycemic foods included sugar, white flour, white potatoes, white rice, white bread, bananas, grapes and melons.

As our goal was not weight loss but helping addicts and alcoholics regain emotional balance and health, restore chronically low dopamine levels and expedite brain repair, we made some modifications. For instance, because many of our clients had damaged their livers by excessive drinking and drug abuse, we chose to exclude pork, a triglyceride that is hard for the liver to process.

We also excluded caffeine because it has drug-like qualities and most addicts drink endless cups of coffee or caffeinated power drinks each day. An added benefit of the caffeine-free diet is that it helped our clients regain their natural sleep cycles.

In the addiction industry, sugar is considered a "transfer addiction," one that complicates issues of brain healing, depression and mood. When addicts stop using drugs and alcohol, they "transfer" their addiction, sometimes to sex or gambling but usually to sugar. Montignac allowed only artificial sweeteners as a sugar substitute when making desserts, and initially we did too. This changed after the publication of some disturbing clinical studies about the harm artificial sweeteners can cause to the body and brain. Now our chefs bake with small amounts of agave syrup and coconut palm sugar, both low glycemic. The desserts are amazing, especially those made with dark chocolate (an important antioxidant) and mature fruit.

Our breakfasts are hearty. Lunch, the meal when beef or lamb is served, is designed to be energizing. Dinner is usually fish or chicken and vegetables. We serve dessert after dinner because the goal is to make our insomniacs comfortable and drowsy.

Whole-wheat and most gluten-free pastas, cooked al dente, can be served at either meal once a week. For those, like me, who crave authentic Italian food, extruded pastas (made by forcing a semolina-and-water dough through a die) can be prepared because they are considered low glycemic: spaghetti, rotini, fusilli, penne, bucatini, macaroni, and rigatoni.

From the day we opened, I witnessed firsthand the dramatic impact our healthy diet had on depressed, anxious people whose addiction to alcohol or drugs was so profound that they were compelled to enter a residential treatment program for 30 to 90 days. In the course of a week, we saw their eyes begin to sparkle, their hair become glossy and their faces regain color. Around day eight, the fog that clouded their thinking began to lift, opening the way for them to go forward with lives that had been all but destroyed by substance abuse.

Public validation came several months after we opened when I accompanied our Malibu Beach Recovery clients to my first-ever meeting of Alcoholics Anonymous. It was crowded; I found a seat next to a total stranger. After the meeting began the secretary asked newcomers who had achieved a landmark in their sobriety — 30, 60 or 90 days — to come forward. When our clients rose, the stranger said to me: "They must be from Malibu Beach Recovery Center — they all look so healthy."

"Wow," I thought, "we are making a difference." I looked around the room; almost everyone else, including those who had put in serious recovery time, appeared downright unhealthy. Not surprisingly, at the break they all drank black coffee and gobbled down sugary cookies.

I decided then and there to prove that there is a link between healthy eating and recovery from addiction and to challenge the existing practice of feeding sugar and carbohydrates to addicts and alcoholics trying to recover. Eight years and about 7,500 meals later, *Malibu Beach Recovery Diet Cookbook* was born. By then I had become a "goal-driven normie" surrounded by so many sober alumni that professionals in the addiction industry had taken notice. Dozens of alumni were waiving their anonymity to go on camera and describe their journey into sobriety. All of them talked about the positive impact of the diet. Those who relapsed came back for what was euphemistically called a "tune up"; the phone

call usually began with a wish to "feel healthy again."

Written with four of our executive chefs, *Malibu Beach Recovery Diet Cookbook* includes four weeks of meal plans, each by a different chef, more than 150 of our tastiest recipes, diet guidelines and shopping lists. We wrote this book for addicts and alcoholics everywhere who are struggling to get into recovery and stay in recovery as well as their parents, spouses, children and friends who are committed to supporting them make the difficult journey to long-term sobriety.

It wasn't the meals alone that helped our clients get sober and stay sober. Treatment included three hours each day of yoga breath work, SynaptaGenX, which is a special over-the-counter supplement designed to raise dopamine levels, and individual and group sessions with our highly trained counselors and therapists. And, of course, they were introduced to the principles of the Twelve Step program.

Recovery is hard. In the first few months, while their brains are repairing, drug addicts and alcoholics are often obsessively resistant to rules. Most treatment centers worry about clients trying to sneak in drugs. Some even have dogs trained to detect drugs. During the years I was owner and chief executive officer of the Malibu Beach Recovery Center, our usual struggle was with clients trying to sneak in unhealthy sugar-laden food as "contraband." We knew they did not need it — the amazing desserts made by our chefs can satisfy the sweet cravings of even the most down-and-out alcoholics and heroin users.

On Sundays I liked to take interested clients to the Malibu Farmers Market to discover beautiful, fresh, seasonal fruits and vegetables. At each stand we would discuss what is "legal" and what is not in terms of the Malibu Beach Recovery Diet. We asked questions about ingredients — sometimes we even texted Licia for a "ruling." We tasted free samples. Sometimes we bought green tortillas made from the cactus nopales and non-genetically modified corn, exotic dragon fruit, creamy cherimoyas and orange or yellow heirloom tomatoes. Before going back to the center, we would visit a stand that served us fresh coconut juice and green smoothies spiked with ginger.

Once a week I still take alumni from our outpatient program to dinner and we practice ordering according to the Malibu Beach Recovery Diet. We start at our local "American-style" restaurants, like Coogie's or Marmalade Café. Once clients get the hang of it, we graduate to Italian and then do a Thai or Vietnamese challenge. These fun outings help clients understand the diet and definitely provide a dopamine surge.

I encourage everyone who is using this cookbook or our website to get out and about and incorporate into their recovery process visits to their local farmers market and interesting restaurants. Starting an herb and vegetable garden in their backyard, or even on their windowsill, will also add pizazz to their new lifestyle.

Regulars at meetings of Alcoholics Anonymous or Narcotics Anonymous are often given what is known as a "commitment." These assignments range from hosting the meeting to greeting arrivals at the front door. Organizing food and drink for the break is an important commitment. Our alumni often call us for "legal" dessert recipes, made with ingredients allowed on the Malibu Beach Recovery Diet, that are healthier and tastier than the usual sugar cookies and Twinkies. You will find many great examples of healthy desserts to serve at Twelve Step meetings in this cookbook and on our website.

Adjusting to healthy eating is not without its challenges. Some of our clients have eaten only fast food for many years. Before working at the Malibu Beach Recovery Center, our beloved Krissie — now a counselor, then a prescription drug addict addicted to pain pills — had never eaten a vegetable she liked. For her and others, our executive chef, Chef Cyril Landrat, overcame his own aversion to foods not based on French culinary traditions and introduced "Fajita Fridays." This high-end Michelin-trained executive chef also poured through fancy cookbooks to satisfy a request for Chinese Orange Chicken. He found a recipe and adapted it to the diet. He was so successful that the clients gave him what for them was the ultimate compliment — they said his Chinese Chicken was every bit as good as the one served at Panda Express.

We also have had clients who, despite their addiction to drugs and alcohol, are bona fide "foodies." I will always remember the client who objected to eating swordfish, afraid it might contain mercury, despite having driven himself to treatment in a car heaped high with used heroin needles. Another asked Chef Cyril to prove his gourmet credentials by serving a French dessert called "floating island," which he did, of course, after adapting the recipe to the Malibu Beach Recovery Diet.

Kenneth Blum, PhD, a very serious scientist who in 1990 co-discovered the link between genetics and addiction, is also a serious "foodie." So serious that the first time he was invited to lunch at Malibu Beach Recovery Center he first stopped for a snack — gourmet enchiladas to be exact — as he was terrified that "low glycemic" was synonymous with boring and tasteless. As you will learn in his introductory comments later in this section, after just one of Chef Cyril's meals, he was "addicted."

About the chefs who helped me write

this cookbook: Licia is known around here as the Dessert Maven. Try her French Chocolate Mousse or her Chocolate Decadence Cake with Raspberry Coulis. Yannick used to own two acclaimed French restaurants. His Seared Flank Steak with Baby Arugula and his Braised Lamb recipes are very popular with our clients, but his Duck Breast and Orange Sauce is one of my all-time favorites. Sergio, who comes to us from Rio de Janeiro, makes the best warm salads in the world and his Brazilian Walnut Cake is to die for. Johnnie grew up in his parents' Italian restaurant, right here in Los Angeles. He has successfully adapted the Malibu Beach Recovery Diet to many of the ethnic favorites that our clients crave, like Jamaican Mango Shrimp, Grandma's Spaghetti and Meat Balls and Chinese Cashew Chicken.

I wish each of you, whether in recovery or helping a loved one into recovery, long-term health and happiness.

Bon appétit!

Joan Borsten
Co-founder, Malibu Beach Recovery Center
www.malibubeachrecoverydiet.com

Malibu Beach Recovery Diet Cookbook **includes:**

- Simple guidelines for incorporating our low-glycemic, high-dopamine diet into your life.
- Four weeks of meal plans, each week created by a different chef.
- 150 of the best and most mouthwatering recipes we have served our clients.
- A list of low-glycemic foods that enhance and regulate dopamine.
- Shopping lists to facilitate entry into the post-addiction treatment world.
- Reports from two of the addiction industry's most eminent neuroscientists who have devoted their careers to understanding the link between addiction and the brain. Mark Gold, MD, and Kenneth Blum, PhD, both explain why a healthy diet can positively impact recovery from alcohol and drug addiction and why normal dopamine levels are a key to sustained good health.

A Healthy Diet Aids Recovery from Alcoholism and Drug Addiction

I am a neuroscientist who has spent over 40 years studying the brain, drugs, medication and addictions. I discovered the Malibu Beach Recovery Center when my colleague, a leading authority on the neuroscience of addiction, Dr. Kenneth Blum, urged me to visit this amazing clinic located in the hills above the beautiful Malibu beaches. I met with the Malibu Beach Recovery Center clinical team and came away impressed with their application of the principles of neuroscience to the treatment of addiction. I have spent a good portion of my adult life visiting treatment centers across the country and had never before come across a center that understood the relationship between recovery from addiction and a healthy diet.

Several months later, I returned to Malibu to host the first-ever meeting of the Addiction and Psychiatry Advisory Board of RiverMend Health, an emerging leader in the field of addiction treatment. The participants in the conference included many of the scientists and doctors considered to be this country's leading minds in the field of addiction and recovery.

I asked Joan Borsten, co-founder of Malibu Beach Recovery Center, to host a reception for the board and to serve some of the food presented in this book. Joan's surprise gift to each of us was a preliminary edition of the cookbook you are now reading.

The innovative theme of the book — the use of food as a tool for recovery — and the quality of the recipes caused this collection of scientists and doctors to ask each other how to promote brain health, recovery and dopamine through diet. This was an important exchange and the discussion continued at our meetings at Pepperdine University the next day.

In the old days, quitting cigarettes was considered healthy, but only to a point. After all, research showed that if you did stop, you might gain weight. Similarly, if you used other drugs of abuse, from alcohol to heroin to cocaine, stopping was commonly accompanied with a craving for junk food and high calories and, again, the result was weight gain. Drug and alcohol treatment centers commonly weaned clients off their addictions with large quantities of rich and unhealthy foods.

I have published a series of studies and reviewed extensively the scientific literature, and it is very clear that drugs of abuse compete with food inside the brain for similar reward pathways. It is also clear that once abuse and addiction set in, food and nutrition become less interesting. But once an addict is successfully detoxified, eating becomes more compelling, often to the extent that overeating, obesity and even food addictions can result. The relationship between drugs and food is so important that most of the premiere treatment centers have started to employ full-time cooks, but what good is it if the clients are simply fed sweets and other high-caloric junk?

By contrast, Malibu Beach Recovery Center has chefs on staff specifically trained to prepare healthy, low-glycemic meals that also enhance dopamine levels in the brain. The quality of the food — reflected in the recipes you will find inside this book — make it hard to tell that the food is designed to promote recovery. Most alcoholics and addicts are known to have low dopamine levels. Dopamine is a neurotransmitter located in the brain that is associated with feelings of well-being. Normal levels of dopamine are regarded as essential in the treatment of alcohol and drug addiction.

All drugs of abuse are liked, wanted, craved and become objects of extreme desire because of their unique ability to make those with low dopamine levels feel good. Addicts and alcoholics self-medicate to stimulate dopamine production. However, the amounts of dopamine released by drinking and taking drugs are many times more than what would be released by talking to a friend, working at a soup kitchen, singing in the church choir, doing a project to successful completion, receiving a promotion, providing support for a loved one and so on.

Healthy food can also change our mood. First, the visual appeal is important — one has to see the food. Preparation whets the appetite and prepares the brain for the reinforcement. (As evidence, just look at the pictures in this book. It is pretty clear that the Malibu Beach Recovery Center chefs are visual artists.) Next is the smell. At the Malibu Beach Recovery Center, the patients live with the chefs and are constantly surrounded by the food and food preparation. Here, all tables are chef's tables!

Last, but certainly not least, one has to eat. When you look around, the patients are eating

with the therapists, neuroscientists, counselors and each other. No one is rushing to be somewhere else. No one is eating like someone will steal his or her food. Everyone is content and, it appears to the observer, that even during dinner they are working on their issues and recovery. In many ways this mirrors the Malibu Beach Recovery Center approach to exercise. Clients engage in yoga breath work, mindfulness exercises, and meditation several times a day. But, always, the exercise is gentle, holistic, and structured to advance the main event: addiction recovery.

In July of 2007, Kelly Brownell (co-author with me of *Food and Addiction: A Comprehensive Handbook*) and I hosted the Yale Conference on Food and Addiction, the first meeting of its kind. This conference brought together for two days 40 experts on nutrition, diabetes, obesity and addiction to discuss and debate the controversies surrounding food and addiction. What emerged were the early signs of a developing field with experts from many disciplines, all of whom were interested in what you eat, how it is prepared and how that food might affect the brain and behavior.

I have devoted my life to the study of food and addiction. While it is hard to summarize 30 years of thinking and hard work, we in the scientific community have shown that manufactured foods have qualities like drugs of abuse. We have even compared self-administration of fructose corn syrup to drugs in lab studies. Animals will self-administer and overindulge in eating fast food or sugary desserts to the point that they look and act addicted.

The Malibu Beach Recovery Center Diet works to fight the impulse to replace one addiction with another. Stop the drugs, but learn how to eat, exercise and live. It is not easy, but Joan Borsten and her team have shown us that it is possible. They have emphasized, as we have, buying local, buying fresh and strategically shopping for the table or next meal.

I am not sure how many will remember the Frito Lay potato chip commercial: "Bet you can't eat just one." Well, that is a problem for many Americans. Food has been engineered and manufactured to have augmented effects on the brain and well-being, but it also has drug-like effects. Eating more than intended, eating when full, eating distorted portions and eating sugary and fatty foods are all part of the modern food addiction and obesity problem.

The Malibu Beach Recovery Diet is really a well-being diet in which food does not stress the person or hijack the brain to induce excesses and different disease states. Successful recovery is all about reasserting individuality and freedoms while addiction does the opposite. Food is an integral part of the holistic recovery process. It is not competitive with the other aspects of the brain-body-spirit work; it helps set the stage for relearning decision-making, weighing risks and rewards, caring about others, feeling empathy, choosing to communicate with language rather than manipulation, suppressing the most primitive emotions and impulses, and giving oneself the time to recover.

The delicious and easy-to-use recipes in *Malibu Beach Recovery Diet Cookbook* have been created, tested and used by the chefs of the Malibu Beach Recovery Center to feed their grateful clients. But this is much more than a cookbook. It is an important statement that diet is a central part of well-being, treatment and recovery.

Mark S. Gold, MD, *is a researcher, author and inventor who has worked for over 40 years to develop models for understanding the effects of tobacco, cocaine, other drugs and food on the brain and behavior. He has pioneered addiction research, treatment and education and is the mentor of many current leaders in the field. Gold began his career discovering how opiate or narcotic drugs cause addiction and where in the brain withdrawal occurred. This theory led to new treatments for addicts, including the use of clonidine and the sequential use of naltrexone. Gold's dopamine hypothesis for cocaine addiction and withdrawal led to a new understanding of cocaine addiction and highlighted the importance of dopamine in drug addictions.*

Professor Mark Gold has lectured or taught at Yale, Harvard, Brown, Columbia, Washington University and the Universities of Florida and Georgia. Gold is the author of over a thousand scientific papers, chapters, abstracts, treatment protocols and manuals for health professionals. Until 2014 Gold was the University of Florida Donald Dizney Eminent Scholar, Distinguished Professor, Chair of Psychiatry and Distinguished Alumni Professor. Prior to that, he was a Distinguished Service Professor of Psychiatry, Neuroscience, Community Health and Family Medicine at the University of Florida College of Medicine.

Are You Getting Enough Dopamine for Dinner?

The answer to the question "Are you getting enough dopamine for dinner?" could be the key in the battle against the tsunami of drug abuse and other addictions that are sweeping the world and particularly America. After decades of research, neuroscientists now recognize that genetics are at the root of many addictions. As they battle to stem the flood tide of abuse, they have come to understand the true nature of food as an addictive substance, a key in the quest for a definitive answer to one of public health's most worrisome problems.

Most people entering treatment for addiction have in common low levels of dopamine, known as the happiness molecule, in the brain. The deficiency can be due to something in their genetic makeup or to diets that are heavy in junk food. Many have no idea what constitutes a healthy diet and a majority seem to have never shared the loving energy of sitting down at the dining table as a true family unit.

Those observations are backed up by research data from functional magnetic resonance imaging (fMRI) and positron emission tomography (PET) imaging, which disclose strong similarities between the ways that drugs and certain foods affect the brain. Reward Deficiency Syndrome (RDS), a concept I developed two decades ago, is based on the recognition that food, sex, gambling and, more recently, internet gaming produce changes in the brain's reward system that are quite similar, if not identical, to those caused by classic substances, including drugs and alcohol. There are also psychological similarities between cravings for food and cravings for drugs.

This body of evidence has marked modern processed foods a prime culprit in the addictive process. Look at how Dr. Mark Gold, one of the world's experts on addiction, sums it up: "We live in a time when food is in abundance, manufactured and available on demand. Highly palatable and so-called fast food can produce effects similar to drugs of abuse."

The similarities are undeniable and they're linked to the levels of dopamine in the brain. Dopamine is a neurotransmitter. In plain language, that is a chemical released by brain cells to send signals to other brain cells. Low brain dopamine produces an aberrant craving that can be directed at drugs, other substances or activities, or food.

Modern, processed food may contribute to the addictive process because sugar induces the release of neuronal dopamine into the synapse (the connection between nerve cells) that is remarkably like what happens with all known psychoactive drugs. Shifting food preferences so that broccoli becomes as reinforcing as, say, French fries, which might work in theory, doesn't work. In fact, the invariable result of encouraging "just say no" as a way of controlling drug- and food-seeking leads to an individual in a depressed state, preoccupied with shame, anger, guilt and denial, with inevitable relapse just around the corner.

The other culprit is in some people's genes. Neuroscience has identified a link between the inability to stop using and low dopamine in carriers of the A1 variant of the dopamine D2 receptor gene. As early as the 1990s, my research established that carriers of this A1 variant (meaning they have 30 to 40 percent fewer dopamine D2 receptors) have reduced brain-reward responsivity, a blunted response to drugs of abuse, including cocaine. Low dopamine function in the brain's hot spot for pleasure leads to aberrant cravings, be they for processed foods, drugs or something else.

If dopamine resistance is the guilty party, what can be done to turn it into enhanced dopamine sensitivity? There are several answers to this important question. One is in what you eat.

Diets high in protein, for example, are known to increase the number of dopamine D2 receptors in the brain. Published works have shown a connection between omega 3, the fatty acid found in fish and plant oils, brain dopamine levels and functionality of dopamine D2 receptors. Fresh fruit contains high levels of tryptophan, an amino acid the body needs to synthesize serotonin, a neurotransmitter involved in anti-depression and reduced food intake. And exercise has been shown to induce BNDF (brain-derived neurotrophic factor), an important secretion influencing the functionality of dopamine.

An understanding of these facts is at the heart of this wonderful new cookbook, compiled by Joan Borsten and four accomplished chefs.

It has grown out of years of refined cooking for clients at the Malibu Beach Recovery Centers, the two alcohol and drug treatment facilities Joan owned with her husband, Oleg Vidov, located in Malibu and Los Angeles. The recipes constitute a novel way of enhancing dopamine sensitivity through honest-to-goodness fresh food, not chemicals. At the centers, clients eat according to the Malibu Beach Recovery Diet and do several hours each day of Kurma Yoga. (Neuroimaging [fMRI] studies indicate that yoga can increase the release of neuronal dopamine into the synapse by a whopping 65 percent).

Malibu Beach Recovery Diet Cookbook reflects an understanding of the power of food and its potential role in enhancing neurotransmitter function and serotonin. Vitamin B_6, which is found in abundance in leafy green vegetables, fish, poultry and whole grains, helps elevate serontin to "feel good" levels. Folate deficiency, which is common in the United States, is often found in patients diagnosed with clinical depression. Insufficient consumption of foods rich in folate (folic acid) can also reduce the amount of serotonin in the brain.

Brain serotonin is important because of its role in the Brain Reward Cascade (BRC), a term I coined in 1989 to show the relationship of brain neurotransmission and dopamine release in the reward site. Serotonin triggers the cascade of serotonin, endorphins and GABA (another neurotransmitter in the central nervous system), leading to the release of the brain dopamine required to feel good. Without brain serotonin, the function of dopamine would be lost as depression and addiction consume the individual.

I am pleased that *Malibu Beach Recovery Diet Cookbook* features many raw vegetables in the daily diet. That's because cooking can destroy the folates in foods that are rich in folic acid, such as leafy green vegetables and starchy beans, including chickpeas, kidney and black beans. *Malibu Beach Recovery Diet Cookbook* also emphasizes foods that have a low glycemic-index rating, meaning they break down slowly during digestion and only gradually release glucose into the bloodstream. The recipes were created by four chefs who recognize the danger of high-glycemic foods that have been associated with diabetes, coronary disease and blood pressure problems.

The answer to the question "Are we getting enough dopamine for dinner?" is a resounding yes for those who follow the Malibu Beach Recovery Diet rules. The recipes in the cookbook, coupled with a program of yoga and agents like SynapatgenX to help activate brain dopamine in the reward site (nucleus accumbens) in order to reduce craving as well as in the relapse site (cingulate gyrus), provide a key for turning a person's life around.

My hat and that of victims of the worldwide epidemic of addiction is off to Joan Borsten and her staff. The Malibu Beach Recovery Diet they have created is a tool whose effect goes far beyond overcoming addiction. It can help give individuals their first chance at being happy and joyful — and sober — for the rest of their lives.

Kenneth Blum, PhD

Kenneth Blum, PhD, *is Malibu Beach Recovery Center's adviser on neuroscience. In 1990 together with Dr. Ernest Noble, Dr. Blum discovered the DRD2 gene, often called the "alcoholic" or "reward" gene. Several years later he coined the phrase "Reward Deficiency Syndrome," now included in many dictionaries. Dr. Blum has devoted his life to advancing scientific knowledge about addiction and the brain and the role dopamine plays in addiction as well as recovery.*

He served for 23 years as Professor of Pharmacology at University of Texas and is currently Courtesy Professor of the Department of Psychiatry at the University of Florida College of Medicine. He is the recipient of numerous awards. Dr. Blum is the author and/or editor of 13 books and has published over 400 peer-reviewed papers. He is also editor-in-chief of the Journal of Genetics Syndromes & Gene Therapy (Omics Group), Journal of Addiction Research & Therapy and Journal of Genetic Diseases & Genetic Reports.

How the Malibu Beach Recovery Diet Works

We created *Malibu Beach Recovery Diet Cookbook* to help recovering addicts and alcoholics regain their health and rejuvenate their body during the recovery process. This diet is also extremely helpful for those with anxiety and depression as well as diabetics and people with eating disorders. In fact, it is a healthy diet everyone can benefit from because it is founded on fundamental principles of good health that enhances well-being.

For the addicts and alcoholics in treatment at any of the Malibu Beach Recovery Centers, healthy eating became a way of life we hoped would become permanent. In view of the incredible variety of foods that can be prepared to satisfy personal taste, our diet hardly seems to qualify as a "diet." There is no large list of forbidden ingredients that instantly leads someone to crave them specifically, whether or not they were fond of them in the first place. With the abundance of foods that are allowed, almost everyone will actually find their culinary possibilities enriched and enhanced by ingredients that were not previously a staple in their diet.

The Malibu Beach Recovery Diet is a new way of nourishing ourselves and supporting the ability of our body to perform at its best. We chose this specific approach because it is based on three key principles: It cleanses our body and allows it to heal itself, it regenerates the functions of our vital organs and it rehabilitates our natural energy and fuels our well-being by restoring the production of dopamine.

1. Cleansing Our Body

Our body has an extraordinary capacity to heal itself. Given the proper support, it will restore its immune system to fight illness, regenerate itself and nurse itself back to health. Unfortunately, not only our own lifestyle and the stress that we experience in this day and age but our personal addictions can deplete our body's capacity to heal. That is the reason why a structured schedule, time for rest and meditation and a healthy exercise program in conjunction with this nutritional program are the perfect combination for a new start.

Our body, unlike our environment, has not dramatically evolved since we were cavemen. We are meant to eat and drink what nature has provided for us and what is at hand according to the seasons. However, due to industrialization, urbanization and globalization, our bodies have had to adapt to the following conditions: chemicals that preserve food so it is available year-round, a growing process that deprives fruits and vegetables of their natural vitamins, hormones that enrich food artificially (enhancing quantity but depleting quality), the increase of serving sizes over recent time, the incorporation of sugar in most of our food, and our own addictions of choice.

The body is naturally geared to heal itself, no matter the circumstances. That is why the state of our health directly relates to the strength of our immune system. The ability of our body to fend off infections, illnesses and stress is directly linked to how our vital organs are able to function. The natural cleansing process occurs at all times, and, if we are aware of what we eat, we can hasten both the detox and the recovery process.

The benefits that are immediately available through the cleansing process can be witnessed in as little as seven to eight days after a client admits into the program, encouraging those in recovery to persevere and embrace the healing powers of this cleansing phase. The body becomes once again devoted to processing food as fuel for energy and can be free of all excessive consumption. In addition, the body can begin to extract all the components of the foods we eat for their specific purposes (such as minerals, vitamins, fiber, protein, etc.) and deliver them in their most potent state where needed in the body.

The cleansing process is aided by:

- Daily consumption of one of the following acidic products at each meal to rehabilitate the pH balance of the digestive system: oranges, lemons, grapefruit, limes, tomatoes and/or vinegar
- A large consumption of ginger and lemon in the form of teas and juices
- Eating when possible only organic foods, organic meats, and fruits and vegetables within their peak season to ensure they contain their maximum potential of vitamins
- Eliminating all chemicals by reading labels

carefully to ensure the food consumed is as natural as possible.

2. Regenerating the Functions of Our Vital Organs

We have to respect the extraordinary programming of our body, a well-oiled machine that serves us well when we take care of it. By knowing how our vital organs function, we can understand exactly what they need for optimum performance. There are key components that we need in our daily diet to support our needs at every level. *Malibu Beach Recovery Diet Cookbook* will show you how to use those ingredients with maximum flavor and ease.

Proteins play a major role in ensuring your health. The primary functions of proteins include building and repairing body tissue, regulation of body processes and formation of enzymes and hormones. Proteins aid in the formation of antibodies that enable the body to fight infection and serve as a major energy supplier. Our body requires proteins for maintenance and healthy growth. There is a constant breakdown of proteins, which is why we need to consume proteins on a regular basis.

Fruits and vegetables provide essential nutrients, vitamins and minerals:

- Spinach contains a tremendous source of vitamin A, a nutrient the human body needs in order to produce cells and tissue.
- Vegetables such as broccoli, sweet potatoes, peppers, cauliflower and peas are excellent sources of vitamin C. With appropriate levels of vitamin C the body is able to maintain a healthy immune system and produce collagen that is critical in the process of binding cells together.
- Mustard and turnip greens are two of the few vegetables than contain vitamin E, which

has proven to be beneficial in increasing blood flow as well as dispersing oxygen throughout the body. The nutrients present in these vegetables also help to defend the body against tissue damage.

- A wide variety of vegetables, particularly legumes such as beans, peas and lentils, contain zinc, which is needed for the immune system to properly work and plays a role in cell division, cell growth and the breakdown of carbohydrates.
- Leafy green vegetables are an excellent source of iron.
- Peas, spinach, beets, asparagus, broccoli, Brussels sprouts, beans and lentils contain appropriate quantities of folic acid, necessary to sustain a healthy pregnancy.
- Cauliflower is one of the few vegetables that contain a nutrient known as vitamin H or biotin. This is essential in helping maintain healthy hemoglobin levels, which transport oxygen to all parts of the body.
- Onions are a great source of silica, a trace mineral that stimulates cell production.

Dairy products such as milk, cheese and cream are a good source of dietary calcium, which is needed for developing strong bones and teeth and for preventing osteoporotic diseases later in life.

Lipids act as energy storage. The body generally uses carbohydrates as a direct form of energy and it stores energy as lipids. When the body has too many carbohydrates to use all at once, many of them are taken to the liver and changed into lipids by special cells. The liver does store some of these, but so do most other cells in the body. Another purpose of lipids is to make up and give structure to the membrane of cells. Substances called phosolipids (which are

half lipids) make up the vast majority of the cell membrane. They also play many other roles in the body, such as providing warmth via insulation, and they act as signaling molecules from cells to other cells.

A few rules apply to maintaining this highly efficient absorption of minerals and nutrients. By respecting the digestive process, we enhance our body's ability to function at its full potential.

- Eat three meals a day at regular times
- Ensure that all meals are nutritionally balanced. Each food group has an impact on our metabolism as described below:

Proteins: Used by your body to build and repair tissue; make enzymes, hormones and other body chemicals; and as a necessary building block of bones, muscles, cartilage, skin and blood. Proteins are found in meats, fish, eggs, nuts, beans, legumes, dairy products and in certain vegetables.

Fats: Some vitamins are fat soluble, meaning fat must be a part of your diet in order for those vitamins to be absorbed. Healthy fats are found in certain fish (salmon, tuna and sardines), nuts, avocado, eggs, seeds and olive oil.

Carbohydrates: Carbs are key for maximum energy, speed, stamina, concentration, recovery and better fluid balance. The best carbohydrates are found in whole-wheat breads, whole grains, vegetables, fruits, milk and yogurt.

The best diet consists of 30 percent protein / 30 percent fat / 40 percent carbohydrates. Some food (fish, eggs) provide both protein and fat, whereas beans and legumes provide both carbohydrates and protein.

- Consume proteins and healthy fats at most meals and snacks. Eating a balance of nutrients will help keep your blood sugar steady and your hunger in check. Vegetables and lean animal sources (including dairy) are your best options for protein. Olive oil, nuts, avocados, seeds and nut butters are healthy fats.

- Drink large quantities of water, preferably not during meals so as not to dilute the role of gastric enzymes during the course of digestion. However, drinking water ten minutes before a meal will make you feel fuller and prevent overeating.

- Reduce your salt consumption as the sodium in salt plays a role in how glucose is metabolized. Rather than salt, you can use spices liberally to flavor dishes, including nature's natural remedies (turmeric, cinnamon, ginger, peppers, nutmeg, cumin, sage, peppermint and garlic).

3. Rehabilitating Our Natural Energy and Fueling Our Well-Being

Introducing into our diet ingredients that boost dopamine production beginning the very first day of treatment is vital. Most of our clients enter treatment with low dopamine levels, which neuroscience tells us is the reason they are self-medicating. Dopamine is the neurotransmitter in the brain that causes us to feel pleasure.

Even while the body is detoxing from alcohol and drugs, thanks to the healthy diet changes will begin to occur that will help recovery and well-being. The changes are both very visible and an encouraging sign of improvement that will further boost your efforts to stay within the parameters of the diet.

As Joan Borsten writes in her introduction to this cookbook, over the past eight years she has observed that within the first 7 to 8 days of treatment "there is a mental and physical transformation" in our clients. Their eyes brighten up and become "alive." The skin becomes rosy and translucent. In addition, the fog begins to lift from their minds. I have noted that their general mobility is more alert, appetite is restored, and cravings are diminished. All of these visible observations support the transformation that is occurring, giving our patients confidence that the process is working. This is due to the foods that are low glycemic and increase and regulate dopamine production in the brain.

The Glycemic Index

Why is the Malibu Beach Recovery Diet Based on the Glycemic Index?

The basis of the Malibu Beach Recovery Diet is the glycemic index. The main benefit of the glycemic index diet is to maintain a steady and stable blood sugar level and prevent extreme fluctuations that lead to mood swings as this is where most addiction relapses occur.

Here is a very abbreviated process of what occurs: Your body performs best when your blood sugar is kept relatively constant. If your blood sugar drops too low, you become lethargic and/or experience increased hunger. And if it goes too high, your brain signals your pancreas to secrete more insulin. Insulin brings your blood sugar back down, but primarily by converting the excess sugar to stored fat. Also, the greater the rate of increase in your blood sugar, the more chance that your body will release an excess amount of insulin and drive your blood sugar back down too low. Therefore, when you eat junk foods or sugary foods that cause a large and rapid glycemic response, you may feel an initial elevation in energy and mood as your blood sugar rises, but this is followed by a cycle of lethargy, more hunger, mood swings and increased fat storage.

The glycemic index is a scoring system that ranks carbohydrates based on their effect on blood sugar levels. Foods high in carbohydrates have the greatest impact on your blood sugar. Other foods, such as fats and proteins, have little effect on blood sugar.

When you eat carbohydrates, they are broken down in the mouth, stomach and intestine into smaller units that the body can use for fuel. These units are a sugar called glucose. Glucose supplies power to every cell in the body. Without it, you wouldn't be alive.

Here's where the glycemic index comes in. Whenever you eat foods that contain carbohydrates, they are completely digested, releasing glucose into the bloodstream. This response is affected by many factors, including the quantity of food, the amount and type of carbohydrate, the cooking method, degree of processing and other factors.

Scientists have learned that different carbohydrate foods cause blood glucose levels to rise at different rates. Some foods cause glucose levels to rise quickly after you eat them. The result is a virtual "gush" of glucose into the bloodstream. Other carbohydrate foods cause glucose levels to rise more slowly — a "trickle," so to speak. The glycemic index is a system that separates the "gusher" foods from the "trickler" foods. By eating less of the gushers and more of the tricklers, you can keep your after-meal blood glucose levels in check.

In a nutshell, the glycemic index is a number scale that ranges from 1 to over 100. Think of it as an automobile's speedometer: When you drive, the higher the speedometer

reading, the faster you're traveling. When you eat, the higher the glycemic index of your food, the faster your blood sugar level will rise; the lower the glycemic index of your food, the more slowly your blood sugar level will rise.

Carbohydrate foods with a low glycemic index (such as whole fruits, vegetables and beans) tend to be healthier, richer in nutrients, less refined and higher in fiber. In contrast, higher glycemic index foods trigger a spike in blood sugar followed by a cascade of hormonal changes, which tend to make you hungry again sooner because they are metabolized quicker than low-glycemic index foods.

How Is the Glycemic Index Measured?

The glycemic index of carbohydrate food is determined by careful scientific testing. All glycemic indexes are ranked in comparison with a reference food, pure glucose. Glucose is what's known as a "simple" sugar. If you were to eat glucose, your body would not have to break it down. Instead, it would go directly into your bloodstream. The glycemic index of glucose has been set at 100.

In order to calculate a food's glycemic index, volunteers eat a carefully measured amount of a test food containing 50 grams of carbohydrates. Over the next two or three hours, blood samples are taken to measure how high the blood glucose rises. They are tested again, in the same way, only this time the volunteers consume 50 grams of glucose (the reference food).

The total rise in blood glucose levels for the test food and glucose are noted and the test food is then expressed as a percentage of the rise from glucose. For example, a hard roll has a glycemic index of 71; this means that when you eat a hard roll, the rise in blood sugar is 71 percent as great compared to the rise in blood sugar when eating a similar amount of glucose. Since the glycemic index of pumpernickel is only 41, you can lower the rise in blood sugar if you eat pumpernickel bread instead of a hard roll. That's how the diet works.

Who Supports the Glycemic Index?

Scientific support for the glycemic index is wide ranging. Since the concept was first developed in 1981 by researchers at the University of Toronto, extensive research from around the globe has confirmed its usefulness. Numerous studies on the glycemic index have appeared in medical and nutrition journals. What's more, the glycemic index is now an important part of diabetes control and is endorsed by diabetes associations in such countries as Australia, New Zealand, Canada, Great Britain, France and throughout Europe.

Factors That Affect the Glycemic Index of Food

Many factors come into play in determining the glycemic index of the foods we eat. Anything that makes it easier for our bodies to convert food to glucose increases the glycemic index and blood sugar levels. As important as it is for our cells to have glucose, it's the rapid gush of glucose into the bloodstream that we want to avoid.

- Starch is a fundamental source of carbohydrate in our diet. Examples of starchy foods include breads, cereals, rice, pasta and potatoes. There are two kinds of starch in food and, yes, you guessed right, one is quickly digested and the other breaks down more slowly. Thus, the glycemic index of a starchy food depends on which is the predominant kind of starch in that particular food. Thanks to the glycemic index researchers, we can make our choices directly from the glycemic index list.

- Cooked foods generally have higher glycemic indexes than uncooked foods. One of the reasons is because cooking causes starches to swell, making them easier to digest. The amount of cooking time can affect the glycemic index, too. When pasta is cooked only until it is al dente (firm), it has a low glycemic index; when pasta is overcooked and becomes soft and mushy, it has a higher glycemic index.

- Highly processed foods have higher glycemic indexes than the unprocessed version. Our staple grains — wheat, corn and oats — are finely ground into powdery flours that produce many wonderful tasting high-glycemic breads, cookies, breakfast cereals and baked goods. For example, old-fashioned oatmeal made from rolled oats has a glycemic index of 49, while Quaker® 1-minute oats has a glycemic index of 66, which raises the blood sugar level 35 percent higher and faster. This means processed 1-minute oats will raise your blood sugar level higher and faster than old-fashioned oats.

- Acidic foods, such as oranges and sourdough bread, have low glycemic indexes. The more acidity there is in food, the more slowly it is emptied from the stomach and, in turn, the more slowly it is digested and turned into blood sugar. Adding acid to a meal in the form of vinegar (as in many salad dressings) or lemon juice can help lower the glycemic index of a meal. In fact, research has shown that adding as little as 4 teaspoons of vinegar in a vinaigrette dressing at an average meal can lower blood sugar by 30 percent.

- Soluble fiber tends to slow digestion, resulting in a low glycemic index. Examples are apples, rolled oats, beans and other legumes. Including kidney beans or chickpeas in a salad or adding an apple as the dessert to a meal will lower that meal's overall glycemic index and thus produce a slower and more subtle rise in after-meal blood sugar levels.

- Fatty foods slow the rate of stomach emptying and thus digestion. Experts agree that daily fat consumption should fall between 20 percent and 35 percent of total caloric intake. The heart-healthiest fats are the monounsaturated and polyunsaturated fats, which are liquid at room temperature. They're found in most vegetable oils and in the fats found in nuts, olives and fatty fish.

- Sugar put in the foods we eat by Mother Nature includes fructose (fruit sugar) and lactose (milk sugar). These natural sugars have low glycemic indexes and will not cause a spike in blood sugar levels. Other sugars, such as sucrose (ordinary table sugar), will spike your blood sugar levels. For example, natural fructose found in fruits has a glycemic index of only 19 compared with a glycemic index of 68 for ordinary table sugar (sucrose). High-fructose corn syrup should be avoided as there is no chemical bond between glucose and fructose molecules in the syrup. Digestion is not required; as a result, the molecules rapidly absorb into your bloodstream, triggering an immediate spike in insulin and immediate production of fats like triglycerides and cholesterol. The take-home message is that not all sugars are created equally.

The Malibu Beach Recovery Diet is the first step on the journey into long-term recovery from addiction, alcoholism, depression and anxiety. Again, it's not a "diet" in the usual sense of the word. As you will see, many wonderful and tasty foods are part of the recipes in this book. What better way to convince you than by showing you the broad variety of foods you can eat on the Malibu Beach Recovery Diet? On the next pages, you'll see a list of the delicious foods you can enjoy as well as a list of foods that are specifically low glycemic and rich in dopamine.

As we say in French, à votre santé!

Licia Jaccard
Chef and Dietary Consultant
Malibu Beach Recovery Center

Foods You Can Enjoy
on the Malibu Beach Recovery Diet

FRUIT

All fruits, including dried fruits and jams made without sugar or grape juice

Exceptions:
- Melons (watermelon, honeydew, etc.)
- Grapes
- Bananas
- Dried dates

VEGETABLES

All vegetables, including sweet potatoes and yams

Exceptions:
- Potatoes other than sweet potatoes, no matter what color
- Cooked root vegetables (beets, carrots, turnips, celeriac, rutabagas, parsnips) Try to eat these vegetables only as one of several other ingredients in a dish — for example, sliced carrots in a beef stew.
- Corn or corn products, including corn syrup, cornmeal, polenta

FISH AND SHELLFISH

All fish and shellfish

MEATS

All meats

Exceptions:
- Pork and pork by-products

EGGS

DAIRY

All dairy

Exceptions:
- Yogurt with whey (use Greek yogurt instead as it is strained)
- Cottage cheese

LEGUMES

All legumes

NUTS AND SEEDS

All Nuts and seeds

Exceptions:
- Chestnuts

OILS

All oils (olive oils must be extra virgin for sautéing)

Exceptions:
- Canola oil

SPICES AND CONDIMENTS

All spices and all condiments, including wine vinegars (alcohol content has evaporated), olives, tahini and salsa

GRAINS

All grains

Exceptions:
- White flour, millet, Israeli couscous

BREAD

All whole-wheat breads, sourdough breads and rye breads

Exceptions:

- White bread, breads with honey, molasses or sugar in composition (always check ingredients of gluten-free breads to make sure they do not include corn and sugar products as they often do)

BREAKFAST CEREALS

Whole bran cereals, steel cut oats and granola

Exceptions:

- Quick cooking oats, bran flakes or any cereal with added sugar

STARCH

Basmati rice, wild rice, brown rice and jasmine rice

Exceptions:

- Arborio rice, white rice, instant rice
- Rice cakes

PASTA

All whole-wheat and most gluten-free pastas, long pasta and ribbon-cut pasta made by forcing a semolina-and-water dough through a die (such as spaghetti, capellini, fusilli, ziti). Pasta should be cooked al dente and may be eaten once a week (read labels carefully to make sure they do not include corn and sugar).

Exceptions:

- Short-cut, decorative-cut, minute, stuffed, irregular extruded pastas that are not whole wheat or gluten-free

SWEETENERS

Agave syrup and coconut palm sugar may be used for baking and in limited quantities for sweetening anything else. Stevia or Splenda may be used to lightly sweeten teas (try to limit to one packet per drink).

Exceptions:

- White sugar, brown sugar, molasses, honey

CHOCOLATE

Any dark chocolate that contains at least 71 percent cocoa can be used for baking and hot chocolate. May also be used for snacking in moderation.

BEVERAGES

All beverages

Exceptions:

- Soda, grape juice or beverages made with grape juice
- Caffeinated drinks (this includes coffee, black and green teas and power drinks). After the first 90 days of sobriety, one coffee or caffeinated tea a day can be cautiously reintroduced.
- No alcohol, beer, wine or fermented drinks like kombucha

Please refer to the Shopping Lists in the back of this book for further information.

Low-Glycemic, Dopamine-Rich Foods

PROTEIN
Chicken
Duck
Eggs
Fish
Other poultry
Red meat
Shellfish
Tofu and most soy-based products

FRUIT
Avocado
Blackberries
Blueberries
Oranges
Papaya
Prunes
Raspberries
Strawberries

VEGETABLES
Asparagus
Avocado
Beets
Bell peppers
Broccoli
Brussels sprouts
Carrots
Cauliflower
Edamame
Fava beans
Kale
Leafy greens
Lima beans
Mustard greens
Peppers
Seaweed
Spinach
Swiss chard

DAIRY
Cheese
Milk
Ricotta cheese
Yogurt – Greek

LEGUMES
Black beans
Chickpeas
Lentils
Garbanzo beans

NUTS AND SEEDS
Almonds and almond butter
Peanuts
Pumpkin seeds
Sesame seeds
Tahini

GRAINS
Oatmeal
Wheat germ
Whole-wheat products

DARK CHOCOLATE

Chef
Yannick Marchand

Chef
Yannick Marchand

I was born in the Maine et Loire region of France known for its rich, fertile soil and the Loire River that runs through it. It provides an especially perfect setting for organic biodynamic farming and viticulture. With my childhood spent under my grandparents' roof, "eating with the seasons" and thriving on our country's vibrant gastronomy were part of my everyday life.

Coming home from school and making a snack from fresh eggs and that morning's batch of goat cheese were things I took for granted, and it wasn't until I came to the U.S. that I realized how much corporate agriculture and processed convenience foods had invaded the modern diet and lifestyle. This realization, along with memories of my grandmother's skilled and gentle touch to cooking, were my inspirations to cook professionally.

After completing my degree at the esteemed New England Culinary Institute in Montpelier, Vermont, I held chef positions at several historic fine dining restaurants in and around New Orleans, before buying and then designing Quatorze Restaurant, which I owned for eight years. Quatorze is a 1920s Parisian Belle Époque-style bistro.

In creating my menus, I have always been honored and blessed to partner with many amazing artisanal local farmers, experiencing firsthand the power of natural quality products on one's physical and mental well-being. And for the last 20 years, I have cultivated a personal practice of yoga — something I find very necessary to help me stay balanced and creative in my cooking and in my entire life.

Week One / Yannick Marchand

So when my friend and associate Cyril Landrat, the executive chef at Malibu Beach Recovery Center, asked me to consider joining his team, I was impressed with the center's holistic approach of using yoga, breathing exercises, and French gourmet low-glycemic cuisine to restore and revitalize the health of patients recovering from addictions. Science can validate which nutrients rebalance our immunity, digestion, and other internal chemistries. I also believe that through the joyful and creative intentions of cooking, we can capture the healing vibrations directly from the ingredients and put them into our bodies in synergistic forms… bringing to life the adage "we are what we eat." I do not believe in complicating our food with man-made chemicals or modified genetics — I simply try to respect and protect nature's gifts as they are and combine their flavors to please our palates. My philosophy is as simple as that.

Breakfast
Lunch
Dinner
Dessert

Monday

Chef Yannick Marchand

Old-Fashioned Steel-Cut Oatmeal with Ginger and Walnuts

Serves 4

Ginger gives great morning energy.

INGREDIENTS

1 cup Irish oatmeal, old-fashioned steel-cut (not quick cooking)
4 cups spring water or filtered water
Pinch of sea salt
1 tsp fresh ginger, skin removed and chopped very fine or grated
1/2 tsp cinnamon, ground (optional)
1/4 tsp nutmeg, ground (optional)
1/2 cup walnuts (optional)

INSTRUCTIONS

In a large pot, add water and a pinch of salt; bring to a boil. When boiling, add the oatmeal, ginger, cinnamon and nutmeg.

Reduce the heat to medium or medium-low and cover lightly. Cook for approximately 20 minutes while stirring regularly to keep the oatmeal from burning or sticking to the pot. It will thicken as it cooks, as the water is absorbed and evaporated. Cook until the consistency is to your liking; remove from heat.

Stir in the walnuts and cover; let it sit covered for 5 to 10 minutes to finish.

To make less or more, simply use a 1:4 ratio of oatmeal to water when modifying the quantity.

Other options: Serve with any other fresh seasonal fruit or spices according to Malibu Beach Recovery Diet's nutritional guidelines. Have fun and be creative with your combinations!

Week One / Yannick Marchand

Marinated Beef Tri-Tip with Pepper Sauce and Root Vegetable Slaw

Serves 4

The pepper awakens the palate and is balanced by crunchy slaw. A good spring-summer dish.

INGREDIENTS

1 lb beef tri-tip, grass-fed organic
3 Tbsp extra-virgin cold pressed olive oil
1–2 Tbsp extra to coat the cooking pan
1 Tbsp paprika
1 Tbsp cumin
1 tsp cayenne
1 tsp turmeric
1/2 tsp fresh ground black pepper
Pinch of sea salt

INSTRUCTIONS

One day ahead, put all dry spices into a small bowl, add 3 Tbsp olive oil and stir. This will be your marinade. Put the meat into a baking dish. With a pastry brush, brush the entire marinade onto all sides of meat. Cover and refrigerate overnight.

Make the Root Vegetable Slaw and your Pepper Sauce. Set these aside until ready to serve.

Remove meat from refrigerator and let it sit at room temperature for approximately 30 minutes.

Preheat oven to 375 degrees.

On medium-high heat, pre-heat a cast iron skillet or any stainless steel pan that can go from stovetop to oven. When hot, coat the pan bottom lightly with the extra 1 to 2 Tbsp olive oil, do not let the oil smoke or burn. Add meat and sear 3 to 4 minutes on each side.

Remove the pan from the stovetop and put the entire pan into the oven for approximately 10 to 15 minutes, finishing the meat to medium or medium-rare, as you prefer. (Exact time will depend on size and thickness of your meat, and how efficiently your pan distributes heat.)

In the meantime, lightly stir-up the Root Vegetable Slaw and adjust the salt and pepper as needed. Give the Pepper Sauce purée (still in the blender) a quick "pulse" for 1 to 2 seconds to re-incorporate everything.

Remove the tri-tip from the oven and immediately transfer onto a platter. Let the meat rest for 5 minutes to allow the meat flavors and juices to settle-in. Slice as thin or thick as you'd like.

Serve with the Pepper Sauce drizzled over the tri-tip and the Root Vegetable Slaw on the side.

Other options: This is a simple but elegant meal. Should you have any leftovers, the meat makes a nice gourmet sandwich the next day, with mustard, lettuce, tomato, onion and anything else that feels right!

Pepper Sauce

INGREDIENTS

> *3 fresh bell peppers (1 each of red, yellow, green; or in any combination of your choice)*
> *2 whole garlic cloves*
> *1/2 cup extra-virgin cold pressed olive oil*
> *Sea salt and fresh ground black pepper to taste*

INSTRUCTIONS

Blacken each pepper over a stove flame, rotate until the entire outer skin is blackened. Put charred peppers in large bowl and cover with plastic wrap to let them steam. After 5 minutes, remove all the blackened skin by gently rinsing all the peppers in lukewarm water. It should peel and slide off easily. When all the charred skins

have been removed, slice the peppers in half lengthwise and scoop all the seeds out.

Put the olive oil, garlic, salt, black pepper and bell peppers into a blender and blend into a very soft puree. If needed, you can add a little more olive oil to make the puree slightly creamy, but you still want the mixture to be "blending like a cascade". Leave in the blender for now and set aside.

Root Vegetable Slaw

INGREDIENTS

Use organic root vegetables whenever possible because they absorb healthy nutrients from the soil.

> *2 large carrots*
> *2 small red and/or orange beets*
> *1 parsnip*
> *1 celery root*
> *Juice of 1 fresh lemon*
> *1 Tbsp apple cider vinegar*
> *Sea salt, fresh ground black pepper and*
> *   cayenne pepper, all to taste*

INSTRUCTIONS

Grate all the vegetables into a large bowl, using the widest size (approximately 1/4-inch) grater. Add the lemon juice, apple cider vinegar, sea salt, black and cayenne peppers and mix well. Adjust seasonings to your liking.

Cover and refrigerate until ready to serve.

Herb Crusted Tilapia and Lemon with Blanched Asparagus

Serves 4

Don't underestimate how tasty tilapia can be. The herbed crust and lemon bring perfect balance to this otherwise bland fish. Blanched asparagus retains the vitamins, and contrasts with the softness of the fish.

INGREDIENTS

4 tilapia fillets, average 6–8 oz. each
1 cup whole-wheat breadcrumbs, plain
1 tsp fresh rosemary, chopped
1 tsp fresh oregano, chopped
1 tsp fresh thyme, chopped
2 organic free-range eggs
2 Tbsp extra-virgin cold pressed olive oil
2 Tbsp unsalted butter
Sea salt and fresh ground black pepper to taste
4 fresh lemon wedges
1 bunch of fresh asparagus, washed
4 cups of filtered water plus 1/2 tsp sea-salt in a large pot

INSTRUCTIONS

Preheat oven to 375 degrees.

Cut off the tough bottoms from the washed asparagus (which is usually a 1-inch section), set aside.

In medium bowl, mix all 3 fresh chopped herbs with breadcrumbs, set aside.

In a separate medium bowl, beat 2 eggs, set aside.

Start bringing to a boil the 4 cups of water with 1/2 tsp salt in a large pot. Separately, in a large non-stick skillet, add the butter and olive oil and begin melting together over medium heat. Be careful not to overheat.

While the butter and olive oil are beginning to melt together, quickly coat each fillet in the egg mixture, wetting all sides. Then dredge only one side of each fillet in the herb bread crumb mixture.

Place the fillets — herb breadcrumb side down — into the skillet. Cook for 1 minute or until the breadcrumbs are light golden. Remove the pan from the stovetop and quickly flip the fillets over. Finish by baking the fish in the preheated oven at 375 degrees for approximately 5 minutes. (If your skillet isn't large enough to fit 4 fillets, do 2 at a time and repeat).

While the tilapia is finishing in the oven, gently drop all the asparagus into the boiling water at the same time. Leave for approximately 60 seconds, or until tender and with slight crunchiness to your liking. Remove and drain in a colander. The tilapia should now be done.

Serve immediately while hot, with a squeeze of fresh lemon, sea salt and fresh ground black pepper to taste. Creatively arrange your platter or plates with the tilapia, asparagus and lemon wedges.

Other options: Feel free to choose other fish fillets, such as salmon or trout, or other vegetables, such as broccoli or green beans. Remember to slightly adjust the cooking times according to the thickness of the fillets. You can also modify your herb mixture according to what compliments the fish you've chosen.

Flourless Chocolate Cupcakes

Decadent, balanced and satisfying.

INGREDIENTS

3 ounces 72% dark chocolate, roughly chopped into 1/2-inch pieces

2 organic eggs, medium to smaller size, beaten in a small bowl

4 Tbsp unsalted butter (1/2 stick), cut into cubes

1/4 cup agave syrup

2 Tbsp spring or filtered water

4–6 fresh strawberries, washed and sliced lengthwise (optional)

1 cup (whipped) unsweetened organic cream (optional)

1/4 cup sliced almonds or minced walnuts (optional)

Equipment: 4–6 silicon cupcake molds (standard size, not jumbo or mini) and a 9x9 or 9x12 baking dish; (it is best to use silicon molds that are heat resistant up to 600 degrees, but no less than up to 450 degrees).

INSTRUCTIONS

Preheat oven to 400 degrees.

In a medium saucepan, mix together the agave and water and whisk together while bringing mixture to a boil. Once the mixture boils, immediately remove from heat and add the chocolate pieces. Stir until melted.

Put back onto low heat and start adding butter cubes, whisk gently and continuously to make sure it doesn't burn. When half the butter has melted, remove from heat and continue mixing until everything is incorporated.

Begin adding beaten eggs a little at a time, continuing to stir with the whisk so the eggs don't "scramble" in your chocolate mixture. Once your batter consistency is smooth, and well blended, pour batter into individual cupcake molds, filling molds 3/4 to the top.

Place unbaked cupcake molds into baking dish, spacing them evenly. Place baking dish into preheated oven. Carefully pour water into baking dish so that the water flows around the molds, up to half the height of the cupcake molds. Be careful not to splash water into the batter. You'll be baking the cupcakes in this "water-bath", referred to as "bain-marie" in French.

Bake for approximately 25–30 minutes, or until a toothpick inserted into middle of the cupcakes is clean when removed.

Remove from oven and place cupcake molds onto a cooling rack for 10–15 minutes to allow cake to settle. Gently remove silicon molds by flexing the sides down, and use a small spatula to lift each cake onto individual serving plates. Serve warm.

Garnish with strawberry slices, nuts and a dollop of unsweetened whipped cream — all optional.

Other options: Choose any seasonal fruit according to Malibu Beach Recovery Diet's nutritional guidelines, or opt to serve without fruit.

Breakfast
Lunch
Dinner
Dessert

Tuesday

Chef Yannick Marchand

Eggs and Broccoli Wrapped in Nori

Serves 4

A good, fun breakfast. Easy to make, too. Impress guests with the simplicity of this recipe. Sesame gives a nice flavor to the scrambled eggs. The Nori Seaweed (buy it in a health food store or a Japanese market) adds minerals and the broccoli adds crunch.

INGREDIENTS

8 organic free-range eggs (2 per person)

4 tsp black or white sesame seeds (1 tsp per 2 eggs)

4 large broccoli stems (1 stem per 2 eggs)

Sea salt and fresh ground black or white pepper to taste

1 to 2 tsp organic unsalted butter (to coat bottom of skillet)

4 large Nori seaweed sheets, one on each plate

INSTRUCTIONS

Wash the broccoli stems and peel outer husk with paring knife being careful not to cut too deep into the edible portion. Once the husks are removed, slice horizontally into very thin circles and set aside.

In a medium bowl, lightly beat the eggs with a fork or whisk, adding in sesame seeds, sea salt and pepper.

Heat a non-stick skillet over medium-low to low flame and melt butter to coat the bottom of the pan. Pour eggs evenly and quickly onto skillet. Immediately begin using a wooden spoon to stir constantly. Stir in small quick motions around entire skillet, making sure to gather the eggs from all areas of the pan, especially the sides and bottom. This will allow the eggs to cook evenly into soft and fluffy curds.

When the eggs are half cooked, add the broccoli bottoms all at once. Finish cooking.

Remove from heat. Using a large spoon, scoop the scrambled eggs onto the center of each Nori sheet and roll (or fold "burrito-style"). Serve immediately — it's important to serve this hot!

Other options: Be creative with garnishes, such as a drop of sesame oil or a drop of tamari (wheat-free) sauce.

Herbes de Provence Grilled Chicken Breast with Ratatouille "Minute"

Serves 4

Herbes de Provence is a favorite French companion for anything grilled. The fresh thyme used in the ratatouille is a good compliment to the diced vegetables.

INGREDIENTS

- 4 hormone free chicken breasts, skinless, boneless (6–8 oz each)
- 2 tsp extra-virgin cold pressed olive oil, poured onto a small plate
- 4 tsp herbes de Provence mixed with a pinch of salt and fresh ground black pepper

Week One / Yannick Marchand

INSTRUCTIONS

Complete STEP 1 for the Ratatouille "Minute". Set aside. Have your skillet, olive oil, salt and pepper for STEP 2 of the Ratatouille "Minute" ready to go, but do not turn on the heat yet.

Preheat the BBQ grill (for the chicken breasts) to high heat.

Dredge each chicken breast (both sides) first in the olive oil, then coat (both sides) with the herbs/salt/pepper mixture.

Lower the BBQ grill heat to medium and place chicken breasts directly onto the grill for approximately 3 minutes per side, depending on size. Rotate periodically to prevent overcooking.

Remove the chicken from the grill and place onto a room temperature serving platter. Check for doneness with a kitchen thermometer inserted into thickest part of each breast, it needs to reach 165°F and the meat should be white (not pink or red) yet still juicy when you cut through.

Finish STEP TWO for the Ratatouille "Minute" (see below). This finishing step will take just "one minute" to cook and your chicken will still be hot.

Other options: Cook chicken in a skillet rather than a BBQ grill.

Ratatouille "Minute"

INGREDIENTS

1 small shallot, peeled and minced
1 clove garlic, peeled and minced
1 medium zucchini, sliced lengthwise, soft inner section removed; diced into 1/4-inch cubes and set aside
1 medium yellow squash, sliced lengthwise and soft inner section removed; diced into 1/4-inch cubes and set aside
1 Roma tomato, sliced lengthwise and soft inner watery section removed; diced into 1/4-inch cubes and set aside
1 small Japanese eggplant, skin peeled entirely using a vegetable peeler; diced into 1/4-inch cubes and set aside
3 sprigs of fresh thyme, washed, leaves hand picked off stems and set aside
2 Tbsp extra-virgin cold pressed olive oil
Pinch of sea salt and fresh ground black pepper

INSTRUCTIONS

STEP 1: The shallot and garlic should be minced, and the zucchini, yellow squash, tomato and eggplant should all be the same size (1/4-inch cubes). Put all these into a bowl with the thyme leaves and toss gently. Set aside.

STEP 2: Heat a skillet on high heat. Add olive oil but don't let it smoke. Add the entire vegetable mixture all at once, letting it sizzle for about 15 seconds. Stir gently with a wooden spoon and sizzle until lightly crunchy. Remove immediately from heat and season with salt and pepper to taste.

Serve immediately with the grilled chicken.

Sautéed Wild Salmon with Eastern Spiced Rice Pilaf

Serves 4

A simple and efficient way to keep salmon from overcooking. The basmati rice is airy and fluffy with a touch of the east.

INGREDIENTS

- *4 fresh wild salmon fillets (6 oz. each), skin removed and deboned if you wish; keep refrigerated until ready to cook, then bring to room temperature for about 10 minutes*
- *1–2 Tbsp extra-virgin cold pressed olive oil*

INSTRUCTIONS

Preheat oven to 350 degrees.

Prepare your Rice Pilaf (see next page): Once you have turned off the heat to let it steam for 10 minutes, it's time to work with your beautiful wild salmon!

Use a large skillet that can go from stovetop to oven, heat on the stove on medium-high heat. Add the olive oil to coat the pan, but don't let it smoke or overheat.

Begin sautéing the salmon fillets by putting them all in the skillet, with the back (prettiest) sides down. When golden brown, flip them over and put the pan into the oven to finish for 4 to 5 minutes.

Remove the pan. Salmon is cooked when you see a little bit of white protein coagulation.

Serve immediately with your Rice Pilaf.

Other options: Feel free to garnish with a sprig of fresh parsley or cilantro.

Rice Pilaf

INGREDIENTS

2 cups uncooked white basmati rice
1 Tbsp shallots, minced
1 Tbsp celery, minced
1 tsp ginger, minced
1 Tbsp olive oil
2 garlic cloves, minced
1 tsp apple cider vinegar
1/2 tsp turmeric powder
1/2 tsp curry powder
2 1/2 cups cold filtered water or spring water,
   mixed with 1 tsp sea salt

INSTRUCTIONS

Using a medium size pot, heat olive oil over medium heat.

Add the shallots, celery, ginger and olive oil. Stir to mix ingredients together, and reduce heat to low, cook gently for 2 minutes. Stir periodically with a wooden spoon (this technique is called "sweating" — to extract the flavors).

Then add the garlic and "sweat" for another 30 seconds while continuing to stir. Be careful that the garlic doesn't burn or it will taste bitter.

Add the vinegar and stir quickly, then add the uncooked rice with the turmeric and curry powders, and mix together well.

Add the water-salt mixture, stir and bring to a boil, then reduce to a simmer and cover with a lid. Simmer for approximately 10 minutes until the water is dissolved but do not let the rice start sticking (or burning) to the pot.

Turn off the heat but leave the pot on the stove. Keep it covered to let the rice continue steaming for 10 minutes while you work on the salmon.

Whole-Wheat Crêpes with Fresh Whipped Cream, Strawberries and Almonds

Serves 4

I discovered at Malibu Beach Recovery Center that this classic French crêpe can be made with whole-wheat flour. A good, fun and easy dessert.

Special tool: 7-inch crêpe pan

INGREDIENTS

3 organic free-range eggs
1 1/2 tsp agave syrup
1 1/2 tsp non-alcohol vanilla extract
1 cup plus 2 Tbsp organic whole milk
3/4 cup whole-wheat flour
1/2 tsp sea salt
Organic butter (to coat crêpe pan)
1/4 cup thinly slivered almonds
*1/2 cup organic strawberries, washed and
    drained (leave top leaves on for now so
    the water doesn't get in)*

INSTRUCTIONS

In a food processor, mix together the agave syrup, eggs, vanilla and milk.

Add the flour and sea salt and pulse for 20 seconds or until everything is well combined. Pour into a bowl that you can cover and refrigerate overnight.

When ready to make your crêpes, use a whisk to gently stir your batter, you want to make sure all the ingredients are evenly blended together without any separation.

Preheat your seasoned crêpe pan over a medium heat. Coat the pan with a small amount of butter using a paper towel — you want to make sure you have an even amount of butter coating the pan bottom and sides. *Hint: keep the butter and paper towel handy — you'll keep using it throughout.

Place your batter bowl as close to the stove as possible and an empty platter for your finished crêpes nearby as well.

Scoop some batter using a small 2 oz. ladle (don't fill to the top). Before you start to pour into the heated pan, lift one side of the pan to a 45 degree angle by using one hand to lift the pan's handle, and the other hand to slowly pour the batter. Keeping one hand on the pan's handle, slowly rotate the pan so the batter spreads evenly and thinly over the pan bottom. *Hint: "thin and even" is the key to great crêpes!

After 10–15 seconds, carefully unstick edges of crêpe with a thin spatula; then lift two edges high enough to grab with your fingers and turn over to finish for 5 seconds. The color should be lightly golden on both sides.

As you work, move your finished crêpes onto the platter. Work quickly and don't be surprised if it takes a few to find your groove! The temperature of your pan may need adjusting, and your wrists need to get used to the motion of rotating the pan at an angle to evenly spread the batter. Re-butter your pan as needed.

Pat dry your strawberries, and remove the top leaves. Slice lengthwise into 1/4" slices.

Prepare your fresh whipped cream. Put a dollop of whipped cream in the middle of an open crêpe, lay a few strawberry slices on top, and sprinkle some slivered almonds. Roll and fill 4 crêpes and serve — Voila!

There should be plenty of batter to practice your art of crêpe-making…be patient — its takes a little bit of practice! You will impress your guests with this — it's a lovely way to finish the evening with a light sophisticated dessert!

Other options: Choose any nuts or seasonal fruit according to Malibu Beach Recovery Diet's nutritional guidelines.

Fresh Whipped Cream

INGREDIENTS

2 cups organic whipping cream

INSTRUCTIONS

Put a large bowl (stainless steel is best) into the freezer for 5 minutes to chill.

Pour the cream into the bowl and using a hand-mixer, turn on to low and begin beating the cream by moving the mixer around the bowl.

When you've found your rhythm, change the speed up to high to whip the cream. Keep moving the mixer around the entire bowl and whip the cream until it forms stiff peaks. Be careful not to over-whip the cream, or else you'll make butter!

Week One / Yannick Marchand

Chicken Sausage and Caramelized Onions with Trio of Bell Peppers

Serves 4

A healthy and well-balanced breakfast. It is okay to add hot sauce and roll it all up in a whole-wheat tortilla.

INGREDIENTS

4 organic fresh chicken sausages
1 medium yellow onion
3 medium bell peppers, one of each color or colors of your choice
3 Tbsp extra-virgin cold pressed olive oil plus more as needed
1 Tbsp apple cider vinegar

INSTRUCTIONS

Bring sausages to room temperature.

Brush off any dirt or debris from the yellow onion, place on cutting board and using sharp knife, cut lengthwise (stem to stem). Remove first layer of outer skin, and then cut off ends (stems). Place each half with flat side down so you can slice lengthwise into 1/4" crescent moons.

Wash bell peppers, peel outer skin with a vegetable peeler, cut in half lengthwise (stem top to bottom), break off the remaining stem ends and remove the inside seeds. Slice lengthwise into thin strips, approximately 1/4" thick.

Heat a large skillet on medium heat (one that can go from stovetop to oven), add 1 Tbsp olive oil and sear the whole sausages. Set cooked sausages aside.

In the same pan add 2 Tbsp olive oil and sliced onions. Cook over medium heat and keep stirring onions — they will begin to caramelize. Add peppers when the onions start to caramelize and keep cooking together. Stir every 15 to 30 seconds so they cook evenly. Add more olive oil as needed to keep everything moist. The onions and peppers should become soft or very slightly crunchy.

Add the sausages to the onion and pepper combination and keep cooking until the sausages are nice and hot, and the onion and peppers are done. Dish onto serving plates.

Next "deglaze" the bottom of the skillet by adding 1 Tbsp of apple cider vinegar and use a whisk to lift up any particles of sausage. Plate the sausages and pour the contents of the deglazed skillet over the sausage, onion and pepper mixture.

Other options: You can substitute chicken sausages with any meat sausages other than pork.

Breakfast
Lunch
Dinner
Dessert

Wednesday

Chef Yannick Marchand

Braised Rack of Lamb and Mint Infusion with Julienne of Raw Carrots and Shitake Mushrooms in Rice Vinegar Dressing

Serves 4

If you have never tried lamb, this is the recipe that will change your mind. If you are already a fan, this incredible dish will impress your guests.

INGREDIENTS

> 1 rack of lamb
> 1/2 cup apple cider vinegar
> 1/2 cup agave syrup
> 1 cup unsalted chicken stock
> 2 Tbsp of reduced chicken stock
>   (available at specialty stores or prepare by
>   reducing 1 cup chicken broth to 2 Tbsp)
> 1 bunch or bouquet of fresh organic mint
> 1/4 tsp Fleur de Sel or to taste

INSTRUCTIONS

Allow the rack of lamb to come to room temperature. Season with fresh ground black pepper on one side only, and set aside.

Preheat oven to 375 degrees.

Start preparing the julienne salad. Using a mandoline, julienne the carrot into 2 inches length, starting with skinny end first and put into salad bowl.

Brush shitake mushroom caps with soft brush or dry towel to remove dirt and particles. Slice lengthwise and set aside.

Heat a large skillet on high heat. When hot, add 1 Tbsp of olive oil and sear the rack of lamb, skin side down until golden brown, which should be 5 to 7 minutes.

Remove rack of lamb from skillet (set aside skillet as is, for the sauce) and put the lamb into a baking dish to finish in oven for approximate 20 minutes but set your timer to 15 minutes to remind you when to start checking for doneness.

While the lamb is finishing in the oven, put the large skillet (used to sear lamb) back on the stovetop. Add apple cider vinegar, stir with a whisk to release the particles at the bottom of pan over a medium high heat. When it starts bubbling, add 1/2 cup agave syrup, stir and let it reduce for 1 minutes on medium high heat.

As soon as it starts bubbling, add 1 cup unsalted chicken stock and 2 Tbsp of reduced chicken stock to help thicken the liquid. Keep using the whisk to mix together over medium high heat, until thickened into a sauce consistency and the liquid is reduced. Remove from heat.

Add 1 bunch or bouquet of fresh mint. Cover and let it infuse for 5 minutes. Pour through a large strainer into a small saucepan so it is ready to warm up over low heat just before serving.

Check on your rack of lamb. It will be ready (medium) when you can push lightly with your finger in the middle of a meaty portion, and it feels similar to pushing on your inner forearm just above your wrist. Remove and put into a resting rack set above a tray so the meat can breathe, and let it rest for 5 minutes.

While your lamb is resting, finish your carrot shitake salad.

Heat a small skillet on medium heat. Add 2 Tbsp olive oil; when hot, sauté your shitake mushrooms. When almost all the olive oil is absorbed, add 1 to 2 Tbsp filtered or spring water, enough to keep the mushrooms moist. Add the 2 Tbsp rice vinegar, stir gently and remove from heat.

Add hot mushrooms to the carrot bowl, season with sea salt and fresh ground black pepper. Toss and it's ready to serve.

Using the more delicate type of sea salt, fleur de sel, season the rack of lamb to taste. Slice each lamb rack with a sharp knife.

Plate and serve lamb rack hot and cooked to perfection, drizzled with your Mint Sauce and the Carrot Shitake Salad on the side.

Raw Carrots and Shitake Mushrooms in Rice Vinegar Dressing

INGREDIENTS

1 large organic carrot, washed and cleaned
4 to 6 shitake mushroom caps, stems removed
1 Tbsp plus 2 Tbsp extra-virgin cold pressed olive oil
1 to 2 Tbsp filtered or spring water
2 Tbsp rice vinegar
Sea salt and fresh ground black pepper to taste

Baked Sea Bass and Tomato, Olive, Parsley Sauce with Chopped Romaine Salad and Tomato, Red Onion, Feta Cheese

Serves 4

Sea Bass is everyone's favorite fish. It is flaky and moist. The simple French combination of olives, parsley, tomatoes and olive oil works perfectly.

INGREDIENTS

4 fresh sea bass fillets (6 oz. each), skin removed if you wish; keep refrigerated until ready to cook, then bring to room temperature for about 10 minutes
1 to 2 Tbsp extra-virgin cold pressed olive oil to dredge sea bass fillets
Sea salt and fresh ground black pepper to taste

2 large whole tomatoes
Medium pot half-filled with filtered water plus 1 Tbsp sea salt (enough to cover tomatoes)
Medium bowl half-filled with filtered ice water
10 Kalamata unpitted olives (this is important for flavor integrity)
2 Tbsp extra-virgin cold pressed olive oil
Pinch of sea salt and fresh ground black pepper
5 to 6 sprigs of fresh parsley whole stems and leaves, washed and dried in a paper towel
Juice of 1/2 organic lemon

INSTRUCTIONS

Remove olive pits by hand, set aside. Mince parsley, set aside. Squeeze lemon, set aside.

Bring water to boil. Remove tomato cores and slice a small cross on each tomato bottom.

Add the tomatoes into the boiling water for 20 seconds, remove and dunk completely into ice water.

Immediately remove the skin of tomatoes, slice in half from top to bottom, remove the seeds, and chop rustically into 1/4 inch or large enough so they keep their shape and do not fall apart. Put into medium mixing bowl, add 2 Tbsp olive oil, a pinch of sea salt and fresh ground black pepper to taste.

Roughly chop the pitted olives into a similar size as the tomatoes and mix gently with the tomatoes using a wooden spoon. Add minced parsley, lemon juice and adjust salt and pepper. Set mixture aside to serve on top of broiled sea bass.

Place sea bass into a baking pan and dredge each fillet with 1 to 2 Tbsp olive oil. Season with sea salt and pepper. Broil for 3 to 4 minutes per side depending on thickness, flip to other side. (Fish overcooks easily, so its best to use a timer and keep watching, it's done when fillets feel flaky and easily fall apart.

Serve fish hot with tomato olive sauce over the broiled sea bass. Serve salad on the side.

Chopped Romaine Salad with Cherry Tomatoes, Olives and Feta Cheese

INGREDIENTS

> *1 head of organic romaine lettuce, washed and dried*
> *1/2 cup of cherry or grape tomatoes, quartered*
> *1/2 small red onion, diced*
> *1/2 cup feta cheese*
> *2 Tbsp extra-virgin cold pressed olive oil*
> *1 Tbsp balsamic vinegar, adjust to taste*
> *Sea salt and fresh ground black pepper*

INSTRUCTIONS

Slice washed and dried romaine head horizontally, 1/2-inch thick. Put into large salad bowl. Add quartered cherry or grape tomatoes, diced red onion, crumbled feta cheese and toss everything together. Set aside.

Finish romaine salad by drizzling in 2 Tbsp of olive oil, or enough so lettuce leaves are slightly shiny, then slowly drizzle 1 Tbsp of balsamic vinegar to taste. Season with sea salt and fresh ground black pepper. Toss again and serve alone with broiled sea bass.

Raw Fruit and Nut Cookie

Serves 4

A good snack to have with you at all times. It is similar to a raw power bar.

INGREDIENTS

> 1/2 cup raw walnuts
> 1/2 cup raw almonds
> 1/2 cup raw cashews
> 1/2 cup dried organic prunes
> 1/2 cup dried organic apricots
> 1/2 cup dried organic cherries
> 2 Tbsp agave syrup
> 2 tsp non-alcohol vanilla extract
> 2 Tbsp shredded fresh ginger
> 1 tsp unsweetened carob powder
> 1/4 tsp sea salt
> 1 Tbsp Bob's Mill almond flour

INSTRUCTIONS

Put all the ingredients (except almond flour) into a large food processor and pulse 5 to 7 times or until mixture comes together as a very chunky paste.

Cover a small cutting board with wax paper and sprinkle almond flour on the surface to prevent batter from sticking.

Scoop all the fruit/nut batter out onto the floured surface, and shape into 1" diameter balls. Flatten slightly and arrange on your cookie tray for serving.

Serve with hot ginger or peppermint tea.

Other options: You can also add 1/4 cup dried, unsweetened shredded coconut to taste. Feel free to substitute any nuts or dried fruits according to Malibu Beach Recovery Diet's nutritional guidelines. You can also substitute lemon or other non-alcohol extract for the vanilla extract.

Breakfast
Lunch
Dinner
Dessert

Thursday

Chef Yannick Marchand

Egg in a Hole with Sautéed Spinach and Garlic

Serves 4

A healthy French version of a classic American breakfast.

INGREDIENTS

2 bags organic spinach, washed
    and drained well
2 cloves organic garlic, minced
1 to 2 Tbsp extra-virgin cold pressed
    olive oil
Sea salt and fresh ground black pepper to taste
4 extra-large organic free-range eggs
4 slices whole-wheat bread
1 Tbsp organic butter

INSTRUCTIONS

Rinse the entire contents of 2 bags of spinach, use a salad spinner to drain as much of the water as possible. Put into mixing bowl.

To the spinach add the minced garlic, 1 Tbsp olive oil plus a pinch of sea salt and fresh ground black pepper. Toss everything lightly but thoroughly.

Prepare other ingredients for immediate use: Set your 4 eggs within easy reach of your stove. Tear out a 1 1/2-inch hole in the center of each bread slice.

Using a large non-stick pan, melt 1 Tbsp of organic butter over medium heat — caution to not let it burn. When melted, place 1 or 2 slices (or as many as will fit) into pan. Let it turn to a golden brown and flip over.

Carefully crack one egg and allow the yolk to drop into the hole of one bread slice. Repeat for each bread slice in the pan. Work quickly so that your eggs will cook consistently. You can season with sea salt and fresh ground black pepper.

Cover, and reduce the heat. Cook until the egg is done to your liking, sunny side up or, if you prefer, carefully flip so the yolks don't break. As each one is done, place onto serving plates.

Heat another skillet on high heat; as soon as it is hot, add spinach mixture and, using 2 wooden spoons, toss constantly for 30 seconds to 1 minute. Remove from heat and place on a serving plate. Top with the egg toast. Serve immediately.

Other options: You can play with different spices to season your eggs differently; try paprika or a little curry powder.

Seared Flank Steak with Baby Arugula

Serves 4

A favorite Italian combination — grilled steak, arugula, Parmesan cheese, olive oil and balsamic vinegar.

INGREDIENTS

1 lb 100% grass-fed flank steak
1 tsp Italian herb mixture
1 tsp fresh ground black pepper
1 Tbsp extra-virgin cold pressed olive oil
Pinch of sea salt
1 bag organic baby arugula
1 Tbsp extra-virgin cold pressed olive oil
2 tsp balsamic vinegar
Sea salt and fresh ground black pepper to taste
Wedge of aged Parmigiano-Reggiano cheese

INSTRUCTIONS

Preheat oven to 350 degrees.

Wash and spin-dry entire bag of arugula. Place into large salad bowl and set aside.

Open flank steak to lay flat in a plate. Season on one side only with the Italian herb mixture and fresh ground black pepper, set aside.

Heat a large skillet (use one that can go from stovetop to oven) on medium heat. When hot, add 1 Tbsp olive oil and sear flank steak with the herbed side down first, for 30 to 45 seconds.

Flip over and move skillet into oven for approximately 10 minutes (if steak is 1-inch thick) or until cooked to medium. You can test by lightly pressing on the steak, it should have a similar touch as lightly pressing on the inside of your wrist. Remove from skillet and lay it out on a resting rack over a tray and season with sea salt to taste. Allow it to rest for 5 minutes.

While meat is resting, finish arugula salad by drizzling 1 Tbsp olive oil, enough so that all the leaves are lightly coated. Add 2 tsp balsamic vinegar, a pinch of sea salt and pepper, and toss well with 2 wooden spoons.

Thinly slice flank steak against the grain. Serve immediately by laying several slices on top of a small serving of the arugula salad. If desired, shave some aged Parmigiano-Reggiano on top of the flank steak and salad.

Shrimp Scampi

Serves 4

The most classic lemony-buttery shrimp scampi ever.

INGREDIENTS

16 medium-size fresh shrimp (peeled, deveined, washed, drained); if you can only find frozen shrimp, defrost and drain excess water

2 Tbsp extra-virgin cold pressed olive oil

2 Tbsp apple cider vinegar

Pinch of sea salt and fresh ground black pepper

6 Tbsp unsalted butter, softened

2 large cloves organic garlic, minced

2 Tbsp organic shallots, minced

2 tsp fresh Italian parsley, washed, patted dry, minced

Pinch of crushed red pepper flakes

1/2 tsp grated organic lemon zest plus cut 4 wedges from the same lemon

1 medium, organic free range egg, yolk only

1/3 cup whole-wheat breadcrumbs, unseasoned

INSTRUCTIONS

Preheat oven to 450 degrees.

In a large mixing bowl, add together the olive oil, apple cider vinegar and a pinch each of sea salt and pepper. Use a whisk to mix well. Add all the shrimp into this marinade and let it sit for 15 minutes. Gently rotate shrimp in the marinade frequently.

While the shrimp are marinating, in a separate bowl combine: the softened butter, egg, garlic, shallots, parsley, crushed red pepper flakes, lemon zest, egg yolk and breadcrumbs. Gently squeeze just a tiny amount of juice from each of the 4 lemon wedges into the mixture. Mix everything well and make sure all the breadcrumbs are moistened and the butter is well incorporated. (Set aside the lemon wedges for later use.)

After 15 minutes, remove the shrimp from the marinade and allow the liquid to drip off. Dredge each shrimp in the breadcrumb/butter mixture, then lay each shrimp flat in a large baking dish; spoon any remaining breadcrumb butter mixture over the shrimp.

Bake for 8 to 10 minutes, depending on the size of the shrimp. Serve immediately with a lemon wedge on the side.

Tomato Cucumber Gazpacho

Serves 4

INGREDIENTS

2 cups organic tomatoes (1 cup pureed, 1 cup
    finely diced)
2 cups organic cucumbers, peeled (1 cup
    pureed, 1 cup finely diced)
1 Tbsp extra-virgin cold pressed olive oil
1/2 red bell pepper, finely diced
1/2 green bell pepper, finely diced
1/2 cup organic celery, peeled and finely diced
Handful of cilantro leaves, washed and patted
    dry, minced
2 tsp fresh ginger, minced or finely grated
1 green onion, washed and minced
A few fresh organic lime wedges
Sea salt and fresh ground black pepper to taste
Optional: 12 to 16 almonds, pre-soaked
    in filtered water for at least a few hours
    (overnight is best)

INSTRUCTIONS

Optional: Prepare almonds by filling a small
bowl with filtered water and add the almonds
to soak. Overnight is best but a few hours can
be okay. Rinse and remove outer skin while wet.
Crush and finely dice the almonds. Set aside.

Using a blender, purée 1 cup of fresh tomatoes
and 1 cup of fresh cucumbers with 1 Tbsp olive
oil. Pour into a large glass bowl.

Add in the red and green bell pepper, celery,
cilantro, ginger and green onion. Stir gently to
allow all the flavors to blend together.

Squeeze the juice of 1 or 2 wedges of lime into
the gazpacho, stir and taste, add more or less
according to taste. Season with sea salt and fresh
ground black pepper to taste.

Cover and refrigerate until serving. Serve chilled.
Garnish with the crushed almonds when serving.

Cinnamon Pot-de-Crème

Serves 4

Pot de Crème is the basis for the French dessert crème brulée (which has a crisp burned sugar top). A perfect classic dessert and easy to make.

INGREDIENTS

> 5 organic free-range eggs
>   (1 whole egg plus 4 yolks only)
> 1/2 cup agave nectar
> 2 cups organic heavy cream
> 1 tsp ground cinnamon

INSTRUCTIONS

Put the 4 yolks and 1 whole egg into a medium bowl. Lightly beat the eggs and agave nectar with a whisk. Set aside.

Preheat oven to 275 degrees.

In a medium sauce pan, mix together the cream and cinnamon and bring to a light boil. Watch it carefully; as soon as it starts a gentle boil, turn off the heat.

Using a small 2-oz. ladle, "temper" the warm cream mixture into the egg mixture. In other words, using one hand for the ladle, and your other hand for the whisk, ladle 2 ounces of the cream mixture while gently stirring with the whisk. This technique of "tempering" allows you to mix the warm cream with the egg batter and not "scramble" the eggs. Continue doing this until all the cream has been ladled into the eggs.

Let the batter rest for 10 minutes. If any foam or bubbles appear on the top, use a flatter spoon to remove these.

Place 4 empty ramekins (2 1/2-inch diameter) into a long baking dish, it's best to leave at least 1 inch of space around each ramekin.

Ladle the egg-cream mixture into each ramekin, filling them 3/4 to the top. Place the dish into the oven. Carefully pour lukewarm water into the baking dish, so it flows around the ramequins and surrounds them 2/3 to the top of the ramequins.

Bake for 35 to 40 minutes, or until the sides are set but the center is still soft.

Remove the ramekins to a cooling rack. Let them cool for at least 1 hour before refrigerating. Serve chilled.

Other options: You can add 1 tsp of vanilla non-alcohol extract into the egg-agave mixture before tempering with the warm cream.

Breakfast
Lunch
Dinner
Dessert

Friday

Chef Yannick Marchand

Vegetable Frittata with Mozzarella

Serves 4

Frittatas are fun because you can use up all of your vegetable leftovers in one dish, adding cheese to give body. Basically a quiche without the crust. Everyone loves it.

INGREDIENTS

6 large organic free-range eggs
*3 cups of any vegetables of your choice,
    either pre-cooked, leftover, or raw*
1/2 cup onion, diced small
1 cup mozzarella cheese, sliced thin
2 to 3 tsp extra-virgin cold pressed olive oil
*1/2 tsp sea salt and fresh ground black pepper
    to taste*

INSTRUCTIONS

This is a great way to use leftover vegetables, cooked or raw, (or any combination is fine). Evenly dice all of them, 1/4 to 1/2-inch cubes and keep the raw vegetables separate from any cooked leftovers.

Preheat oven to 350 degrees.

Heat a large cast iron pan (or large skillet that can go from stovetop to oven) over medium high heat. When your pan is hot, add 1 tsp of olive oil with the raw diced onions, sauté for 1 minute, and add another 1 to 2 tsp of olive oil with any raw diced vegetables

Sauté until everything it is just tender. If you are using any pre-cooked vegetables, add those in

and stir quickly to briefly heat up. Remove from heat and set aside while you prepare your eggs.

In a medium bowl, beat 6 eggs with a whisk until fluffy, add 1/2 tsp sea salt and several dashes of fresh ground black pepper; keep whisking to incorporate a lot of air. This will help your eggs "puff up" when you are finishing them in the oven.

Make sure the vegetable pan has enough olive oil to prevent sticking; drizzle in a little more olive oil if needed. Add your eggs and give a quick stir to evenly distribute everything. Lay the mozzarella cheese evenly across the top.

Cover with the appropriate heat-resistant lid and bake for 10 to 15 minutes, or until done. The frittata will puff up and rise.

Remove the pan from the oven (remember the handle is hot!) and allow it to cool for several minutes. Slice like a pie and serve hot.

Other options: Experiment with different combinations of vegetables, or diced meats, according to the Malibu Beach Recovery Diet's nutritional guidelines. You can also substitute goat cheese for the mozzarella. Goat cheese makes a great complement with spinach, onions and garlic.

Remember that the quality and freshness of your eggs makes a huge difference. Always choose organic free-range eggs; your local farmer's market is a great place to buy your eggs.

Beef Burger with Green Tomatillo Salsa and Cucumber Dill Yogurt Salad

Serves 4

The classic American hamburger made with healthy grass-fed beef. I created a fresh tomatillo salsa to use instead of ketchup and paired with a refreshing cucumber salad.

INGREDIENTS

Burgers

1 lb ground beef, 100% grass-fed (grass-fed raised and finished), hand-shaped into four 4-oz patties
4 whole-wheat buns
4 large lettuce leaves, washed and dried
4 large tomato slices
4 large red onion slices
Extra-virgin cold pressed olive oil (have a bottle handy, to use as needed)
Sea salt and fresh ground black pepper to taste

Green Tomatillo Salsa

6 medium tomatillos
1 whole small Serrano pepper
1 Tbsp red onion, chopped
1 handful of fresh cilantro leaves, washed and drained
1 clove raw garlic
Juice of 1 organic fresh lime
Extra-virgin cold pressed olive oil if necessary
Sea salt and fresh cracked pepper to taste

Organic Cucumber, Dill Yogurt Salad

1 organic English cucumber, skin removed with a peeler
1 tsp sea salt
1 cup plain Greek style organic yogurt
1 Tbsp fresh chopped dill
1/4 tsp fresh ground black pepper

INSTRUCTIONS

Pickle cucumbers: Remove the skin from the cucumber, slice lengthwise in half and use a tiny spoon to remove the seeds. Slice horizontally into 1/4-inch thin half-moons (use a mandolin if you have one) and put all the slices into a large strainer or colander. Toss well with 1 tsp sea salt and immediately set the strainer over a bowl to collect the liquid. Refrigerate until chilled.

Remove your cucumbers from the strainer and combine with the Greek yogurt and chopped dill into a large serving bowl. Season with fresh ground black pepper. Toss well and adjust seasonings if needed and set aside.

Shape your burger patties, evenly season both sides with sea salt and fresh ground black pepper and set aside on a plate.

Put all the ingredients for the Green Tomatillo Salsa into a blender or food processor. Starting on low speed or pulse, mix everything and gradually switch to high speed to make a purée. If the salsa is too thick to blend properly (which happens if the tomatillos are not juicy enough), simply add a little olive oil to help the blender work smoothly. Pour into a serving bowl and season to taste with sea salt and pepper. Set aside.

Preheat grill to medium heat.

Brush the patties with a little olive oil on both sides. Place the patties onto the hot grill for 4 to 5 minutes on each side, or until done to your liking. (Caution for any fat that is dripping onto the grill flames.)

If you are using the stove, heat a large cast iron skillet on medium heat; when hot, add your patties. (Caution for any fat that may splash). Cook 4 to 5 minutes on each side, or until done.

Optional: If you'd like, warm your whole-wheat buns on the grill or in the oven while your burgers are cooking.

Build your juicy burgers with the lettuce, tomato and onion, topped with your Green Tomatillo Salsa. Serve the Cucumber Dill Yogurt Salad on the side. Substitute or add any condiments or dressings, according to Malibu Beach Recovery Diet's nutritional guidelines.

Other options: Any leftover salsa should stay fresh for 5 to 7 days in the refrigerator. Any leftover cucumber salad will release more water so you can just drain the excess before serving.

Cod Cakes with Butter Lettuce and Dijon Vinaigrette

Serves 4

This is my version of a delicious French fish dish adapted for a low-glycemic diet. Don't be afraid of trying it. So good.

INGREDIENTS

Cod Cakes
> 1 pound wild cod (any type of cod fish)
> 2 whole organic sweet potatoes, medium size
> 1 tsp fresh organic parsley, washed and minced
> 1 tsp organic yellow onion, minced
> 1 organic free-range large egg
> 1 cup whole-wheat plain breadcrumbs
> 1 Tbsp organic unsalted butter
> 1 Tbsp extra-virgin cold pressed olive oil
> 1/2 tsp sea salt
> 1/2 tsp fresh ground black pepper

Butter Lettuce and Dijon Vinaigrette
> 1 head organic butter lettuce, leaves washed and dried
> 1 Tbsp Dijon mustard
> 1 tsp organic shallot, minced
> Juice of 1 small organic lemon
> 1 cup (plus extra 1/2 cup as needed) extra-virgin cold pressed olive oil
> Sea salt and fresh ground black pepper to taste

INSTRUCTIONS

Wash and dry the butter lettuce leaves. Set aside.

Prepare your salad vinaigrette: In a medium size salad serving bowl, add the Dijon mustard, the lemon juice and shallots, mix together.

Using a whisk, gradually mix in 1 cup of olive oil — it is important to pour the oil in very slowly as you whisk — this technique will create the necessary emulsion. Add up to another 1/2 cup of olive oil as needed to get the proper consistency. Finish by seasoning with sea salt and fresh ground black pepper to taste. Set aside and refrigerate.

Cut the cod into 1-inch cubes, set aside.

Using a separate large pot, boil the sweet potatoes in filtered water with a pinch of sea salt. Boil until soft, remove the potatoes (but keep the water); allow the potatoes to cool and drain in a colander.

Using the water from the potatoes, bring the water to a gentle simmer (medium high heat). Poach the cod pieces by gently laying them in the water with a large slotted spoon, approximately 2 minutes. Using the large slotted spoon, quickly remove them and allow the cod to drain in a strainer.

Remove the skin from the cooled potatoes. Roughly cut the potatoes into cubes and put into a large mixing bowl.

Add the drained cod, minced parsley, onions, egg, and 1/2 cup of the breadcrumbs; then add 1/2 tsp sea salt and 1/2 tsp fresh ground black pepper. Mix and mash everything together with a large fork utensil. With clean hands, form 2-inch diameter balls and set aside.

On a large plate, pour the remaining 1/2 cup of breadcrumbs. Flatten the balls half way and dredge in breadcrumbs.

Heat a large skillet with 1 Tbsp butter and 1 Tbsp olive oil. Pan fry the cod cakes until golden brown, flip and finish until both sides are golden brown. Remove from the pan and place onto serving platter. Serve hot.

When ready to serve, remove your vinaigrette from the refrigerator, if the dressing has thickened, you can sprinkle a few drops of warm water and toss with the lettuce leaves.

Tomato Basil Garlic Soup

Serves 4

This is a French potage (thick soup). We use olive oil instead of cream to give it body and thickness. Can be served hot or cold, and also the next day as a first course.

INGREDIENTS

1 cup of homemade croutons, using whole-wheat bread or baguette, cut into 1/2-inch cubes

4 large organic tomatoes, washed

1/2 medium organic yellow onion

2 cloves organic garlic

4 cups organic chicken stock

1 bunch organic fresh basil

Extra-virgin cold pressed olive oil, (have a bottle handy, to use as needed)

Sea salt and fresh ground pepper to taste

INSTRUCTIONS

Preheat oven to 350 degrees.

To make your homemade croutons, place 1 cup bread cubes on a baking sheet or pan, drizzle with a little olive oil to coat, toss with a pinch of sea salt and toast in the oven for 15 to 20 minutes. Check and re-toss as needed, until golden brown on all sides. Remove the croutons from the sheet pan and set aside to cool.

Place the whole tomatoes, the half onion and garlic cloves onto the same baking pan that you used to toast the croutons. Drizzle with olive oil. Roast in the oven for 20 minutes.

When the vegetables are roasted, remove them from the oven and put everything into a large pot. Add 4 cups of chicken stock, bring to a boil, and then simmer for another 15 minutes.

Adjust the seasoning with sea salt and black pepper to taste. Pour into a blender, add the basil and purée into a soup. (You can do this in 2 batches if your blender isn't large enough.) Add everything back into the pot and set aside. Serve hot with croutons on top.

Almond-Crust Cheesecake

Serves 4-6

We substituted an almond crust for the usual graham cracker crust to make our own version of a classic cheesecake.

INGREDIENTS

- 2 cups soaked almonds; best to soak overnight, rinse and drain
- 3 Tbsp unsalted organic butter
- 3 packages (8-oz each) organic cream cheese
- 3 medium organic free-range eggs
- 1/2 cup agave syrup
- 1 Tbsp non-alcohol vanilla

INSTRUCTIONS

Preferably the night before, soak 2 cups almonds in filtered water. Make sure the almonds are completely submerged.

Preheat oven to 375 degrees.

Rinse the almonds and drain as much water as possible.

Melt butter and combine with the soaked and drained almonds in a food processor. Use the pulse setting to mix everything together. Be careful not to over mix, you want the mixture to stick together when pressed, but still have a slight crumbly texture.

Scoop the mixture into a springform pan, evenly spread along the pan bottom first, then up the sides. Press lightly to keep the thickness even all around. Set aside.

Wash and dry the food processor, add the cream cheese, eggs, agave syrup and vanilla into the food processor and blend until smooth. Pour into pan over the almond crust mixture.

Wrap the outside of the pan with aluminum foil to prevent the oils from leaking. Place on a sheet pan and bake for 35 to 40 minutes, or until toothpick inserted into the middle comes out clean.

Let it cool before unlocking the spring form pan. Served chilled.

Other options: You can top with a few blueberries or other fruit according to the Malibu Beach Recovery Diet's nutritional guidelines.

Breakfast
Lunch
Dinner
Dessert

Saturday

Chef Yannick Marchand

Eggs Poached in Tomato Sauce over English Muffins with Turkey Bacon

Serves 4

Our version of the popular English breakfast.

INGREDIENTS

4 extra-large organic free-range eggs, at room temperature

1/2 yellow onion, diced small

1/4 cup organic carrots, diced small

2 garlic cloves, minced

2 tsp fresh thyme leaves, wood stems discarded

1 can (28-oz) whole peeled tomatoes

2 whole-wheat English muffins (one half muffin per person)

8 slices organic turkey bacon, nitrate-free

3 Tbsp extra-virgin cold pressed olive oil

Sea salt and fresh ground black pepper to taste

INSTRUCTIONS

Preheat oven to 350 degrees.

In a medium pot, add the olive oil. When hot, add the diced carrots and onions to "sweat" (extract flavors) for 2 to 3 minutes, until the onions are transparent. Add the thyme leaves and garlic, stir slowly for 1 minute.

Add the entire can of whole tomatoes by pouring all the liquid in and crushing the whole tomatoes with your hand before dropping into the pot. Make sure all the tomatoes are well crushed, stir everything together and bring to a boil.

Add a pinch of sea salt and black pepper. Stir and reduce to a simmer, then cover to simmer for 20 to 25 minutes.

Lay the turkey bacon slices in a baking dish and bake until crispy; follow the turkey bacon package instructions.

Remove the tomato sauce from heat and pour into a blender. Set aside the pot to use later. Purée the mixture until all the vegetables are blended together into a sauce consistency. Add the tomato sauce back into the pot and put back onto a medium heat.

Open the English muffins so you have four halves. Toast all muffin halves to a medium crispiness and put each toasted half onto separate plates for serving.

Adjust the heat for the tomato sauce to low, carefully break each egg into the hot tomato sauce to poach whole. Cover and poach for 2 minutes or until it is done to your liking. The dish works well with the yolk intact and a little runny inside, but cook to your preference. Spoon one poached egg onto one muffin half and ladle a generous amount of tomato sauce over it.

Serve the muffin and poached egg with sauce right away, with two warm turkey bacon slices.

Fish Tacos with Young "Nopales" Cactus Salad

Serves 6

This is my version of Baja fish tacos. The salad of nopales is full of protein and tasty, too.

INGREDIENTS

4 medium whole-wheat tortillas
2 tilapia fillets
1 organic egg
2 cups whole-wheat breadcrumbs
Sea salt and fresh ground black pepper
2 Tbsp extra-virgin cold pressed olive oil
1 Tbsp butter
1 cup of shredded cabbage

Salsa
1 tomato, diced small
1/2 Serrano pepper, minced
2 tsp minced red onion
Juice 1/2 fresh organic lime
1/4 cup fresh cilantro leaves (stems removed)
1 Tbsp extra-virgin cold pressed olive oil
Sea salt and fresh ground black pepper

Young Nopales Cactus Salad
1 cup dried adzuki beans, soaked overnight, rinsed and drained
1/2 red onion, diced
1 garlic clove, minced
1 young nopales cactus leaf, small (about 4 by 4 inch), wash and remove thorns
1/2 cup cilantro leaves
Juice of 1/2 lime
2 Tbsp extra-virgin cold pressed olive oil
Sea salt and fresh ground pepper

INSTRUCTIONS

Soak the adzuki beans overnight.

Rinse and drain the adzuki beans and put into pot with 4 cups filtered water and 1 tsp sea salt. Bring to boil; once it starts boiling, cover and reduce to simmer for 45 minutes or until beans are tender. Stir occasionally, make sure there is enough water and that the beans are not sticking. When done, drain in a colander and set aside.

Mince your onion and garlic and set aside.

Fill a large bowl with ice water and set aside. Fill another medium pot halfway with filtered water and 1 tsp sea salt. Bring to rapid boil, add the cactus leaf (make sure its completely covered) and blanch for 30 to 45 seconds. The cactus leaf should be slightly soft if you insert a small knife. Leave the water in the pot but remove the cactus leaf. Put the cactus immediately into the ice bath to stop the cooking and keep its bright color. After 15 seconds or once it is cooled, remove from ice bath and dry, so it doesn't absorb the water. Set aside.

In a large serving bowl mix together and toss the minced red onion and garlic, cilantro leaves and adzuki beans. Add 2 Tbsp olive oil and toss again to coat everything well. Season with sea salt and pepper. Refrigerate.

In a medium sized bowl, crack the egg and beat well with a fork. Slice each tilapia fillet into 4 strips lengthwise (8 strips total), and put into the egg bowl. Refrigerate and turn fillets over periodically so the egg evenly coats each strip.

For your salsa dressing, dice the tomato and put into a mixing bowl with the minced red onion. Then mince the half Serrano pepper (with its seeds) very, very finely; add to diced tomato. (Be careful not to touch your eyes or face; wash the cutting board and hands really well.) Add a pinch of sea salt and black pepper, the lime juice, and cilantro leaves. Drizzle in 1 Tbsp olive oil, mix and set aside.

Shred the cabbage into a serving bowl and set aside.

Remove fish from refrigerator. Spread the breadcrumbs on a large flat plate next to the stove. Set both up next to stove.

Now finish your Cactus Salad: remove the adzuki bean mixture from the refrigerator. Dice the cactus leaf into 1/4-inch cubes and add to salad mixture. Toss gently and readjust seasoning and olive oil as needed. Set aside for serving.

Put a nonstick pan on medium heat, add 2 Tbsp olive oil and 1 Tbsp unsalted butter; allow to melt together to coat the pan bottom.

Coat the tilapia on all sides with the breadcrumbs. Lay the tilapia strips flat in the hot pan, and let them cook 2 minutes on each side. Monitor carefully to not let the breadcrumbs burn. Transfer the finished tilapia to a serving platter.

Warm tortillas over low flame (place directly on stove grills) and put on a large plate, covered with a clean lightweight towel or napkin.

Each person can fill their own taco with 2 tilapia strips, shredded cabbage and homemade salsa. Serve the Young Cactus "Nopales" Salad on the side.

Other options: Add any grated organic cheese, according to the Malibu Beach Recovery Diet's nutritional guidelines. Or, use a jumbo size whole-wheat tortilla and wrap/fold it around the tilapia, shredded cabbage and cactus salad inside to make a burrito.

Duck Breast and Orange Sauce with Spicy Green Beans

Serves 4

"Canard à l'Orange" is Joan's favorite dish. I modified it to fit the diet. You'll never know the difference. It pairs perfectly with the eastern-style green beans. The orange flavor and spices in the green bean dish balance well.

INGREDIENTS

Duck

    4 duck breasts, with skin on

    4 cups fresh-squeezed organic orange juice

    Sea salt and fresh ground black pepper to taste

Spicy Green Beans

    1/2 pound French green beans, rinsed and trimmed

    2 Tbsp olive oil

    2 tsp fresh organic ginger, minced

    2 cloves organic garlic, minced

    1 tsp cumin powder

    1 tsp ground coriander

    1/4 tsp cayenne powder

    2 Tbsp extra-virgin cold pressed olive oil

    5 cups filtered water

    1 tsp sea salt

Week One / Yannick Marchand

INSTRUCTIONS

Squeeze 4 cups of juice from the oranges and set aside.

In a medium pot, add 5 cups of filtered water with 1 tsp sea salt. Bring to a rapid boil and add all the green beans. Once the water comes back to a boil, blanch the beans for 2 minutes (use a timer to be exact). Setup a colander in the sink to prepare to drain the beans. As soon as the timer rings, remove from heat and carefully pour the beans and hot water into the colander to drain. Heat a large pan on medium heat; when hot, add 2 Tbsp olive oil and reduce to low heat. Immediately add the minced ginger and blanched green beans.

Cook for 1 minute then add the minced garlic, cumin, coriander and cayenne. Stir quickly and cover for approximately 2 more minutes, stirring occasionally, until the beans are barely tender. If the spices and beans get sticky, add a little spring water to help mix everything together. Turn off the heat and remove the lid. Set aside.

Preheat oven to 375 degrees.

Place duck breasts skin side down on a non-slip cutting board. Using a small paring knife, remove the silver part of the skin.

Heat a large cast-iron skillet on medium heat. When hot, place duck breasts skin-side down. Season with sea salt and black pepper. As the duck cooks, it will release a lot of fat from the skin. Use a large spoon to remove the liquid fat from the skillet — this technique is called "rendering the fat" from the duck skin and helps the skin come to a crisp texture.

After rendering exactly 3 times, remove the duck breasts from the skillet and place in a baking pan (set aside the skillet as is).

Finish the duck in the preheated oven for 5 to 7 minutes, or until skins are perfectly crispy but the meat is still tender and juicy.

Put the skillet back onto high heat. Remove any remaining liquid fat from the duck skin but leave the crispy particles in the skillet. Pour in the orange juice. Use a whisk to stir and lift the crispy particles from the pan bottom. This is called deglazing your pan. Keep whisking, as the liquid reduces down to half, thickened to a sauce consistency. Season with sea salt and pepper.

While your sauce continues to reduce, check your duck. When done, remove the duck from the oven and let rest on a rack for 5 minutes.

Quickly reheat the green beans on medium heat for 1 minute. Serve hot with the duck and orange sauce. Slice duck breasts at a slight angle and plate. Drizzle orange sauce around the duck slices and serve with the Spicy Green Beans.

Other options: Feel free to save all the liquid duck fat for future recipes that call for duck fat. A little bit can add a lot of flavor. You can put the cooled fat into a glass jar, seal tightly with a lid, and store in the refrigerator. Use within several weeks.

Poached Pears with Vanilla Syrup

Serves 4

This dessert will satisfy your sweet tooth. To make it fancier, add to the syrup during the last 5 minutes some goji berries, chopped almonds or walnuts.

INGREDIENTS

4 whole Bosc pears, choose pears with a light firmness, wash and dry
1/2 cup agave syrup
3 cups filtered water
1 whole fresh vanilla bean
2 star anise cut in 2 pieces - 4 total
1 cinnamon stick

INSTRUCTIONS

Delicately remove the thin pear skins with a peeler but leave the top stem in tact. Gently carve out the bottom stem with a paring knife. This will help the water seep all the way into the pears during the poaching process.

In a medium pot, add filtered water and agave and bring to a boil.

Slice vanilla bean lengthwise to split open, set aside.

Reduce to a simmer, add the star anise and cinnamon stick, scrape the inside of the vanilla bean and add both the entire insides and outer pod to the simmering water.

When the agave syrup and water are well incorporated add all 4 pears. They must be submerged so use a heat resistant dish or all metal small pot lid to gently lay in the pot on top the pears to help keep them submerged.

Simmer on low heat for 30 to 45 minutes or until the pears are tender (depends on size). Remove the pears from pot but keep the pot on the flame and turn up to medium high heat.

Set the poached pears aside to drain any excess water. Using the poaching liquid to make a sauce, allow the liquid to reduce to syrup consistency. Stir regularly to keep from burning.

When done, plate your pears and pour the spice syrup over the whole poached pears. Decorate with pieces of the spices. Serve warm.

Other options: Add some goji berries, chopped almonds or walnuts during the last 5 minutes.

Breakfast
Lunch
Dinner
Dessert

Sunday

Chef Yannick Marchand

French Omelette with Chives and Goat Cheese

Serves 4

Easy and elegant.

INGREDIENTS

> 8 organic free-range eggs
> 4 Tbsp fresh chives
> 4 Tbsp fresh goat cheese
> 2 Tbsp organic unsalted butter, softened
> Extra-virgin cold pressed olive oil
> Sea salt and fresh ground black pepper to taste

INSTRUCTIONS

Preheat oven to 350 degrees.

Set up your "omelette station" near your stove. Divide the minced chives and goat cheese into 4 portions each. Break 2 eggs in a small bowl and beat with a fork for at least 2 minutes to add air so the omelette will be softer and fluffier; mix in 1 Tbsp of the minced chives.

Place a small non-stick pan on high heat for 10 to 15 seconds, and then reduce to medium heat. Add 1 1/2 tsp butter to coat the pan bottom but make sure it doesn't burn; if it does, it indicates the pan is too hot so move the pan off to the side for few seconds.

Have a wooden spoon in your hand and pour the eggs from the bowl onto the pan. With the wooden spoon, immediately begin moving the eggs around with small and rapid wrist movements, for 5 to 10 seconds. The trick is in the wrist; relax the wrist and move the spoon quickly and in short movements; work your way around the entire pan, including the sides. The omelette should start to take shape into "fluffy-looking curdles".

Remove from heat, crumble the 1 Tbsp goat cheese all over on top.

Place pan into the preheated oven for 30 to 45 seconds. When done, the cheese should be mostly melted and the eggs should be soft but cooked and ready to fold over in half. Slide out onto a plate and repeat for the other omelettes.

Plate and serve each omelette immediately. A beautiful omelette may take a little practice — remember, the key is to relax the wrist!

Other options: You can substitute any cheese or vegetable that you'd like; just prepare your ingredients in a "mise en place" — setting up your work station so everything is prepared and ready to go before you start cooking.

Caesar Salad with Lemon Dijon Dressing

Serves 4

This is a quick and satisfying version of Caesar salad.

INGREDIENTS

1 small head of organic romaine lettuce
1 Tbsp Dijon mustard
Juice of 1 organic lemon
1 cup of extra-virgin cold pressed olive oil
Sea salt and fresh ground black pepper to taste

INSTRUCTIONS

Roughly chop the romaine head, rinse and spin dry. Set aside.

In a large serving bowl, add the Dijon mustard and lemon juice and whisk together. Add a pinch of sea salt and fresh ground black pepper and mix. Then, slowly start drizzling 1 cup of olive oil while you simultaneously whisk with the ingredients. The moment all the ingredients are emulsified into a dressing consistency, stop whisking immediately or the dressing will "break". Adjust the seasoning if necessary.

Add all the chopped romaine into the dressing bowl, toss lightly with a large fork and large spoon until all the leaves are covered with dressing. Serve immediately once dressed.
Tip: if the emulsification breaks, in other words, the oil separates from the rest of the dressing, pour everything into an empty jar with a lid. When ready to serve, shake vigorously and pour over the lettuce leaves.

Week One / Yannick Marchand

Three-Cheese Pizza with Fresh Rosemary

Serves 4

This is a classic American-style Italian pizza. It's pretty easy to make the crust. You can also buy whole-wheat pizza dough at Trader Joe's.

Note: You will need a large mixing bowl (glass or metal), at least one clean dry kitchen towel and a dry working surface to knead and roll your dough. Also, a pizza stone is useful but not required.

INGREDIENTS

Pizza Dough
3/4 cup warm filtered water
1 tsp organic whole milk
2 tsp active dry yeast
2 cups organic whole-wheat flour plus
    extra to flour your working surface
1/2 tsp sea salt
1 Tbsp extra-virgin cold pressed olive oil plus
    extra to coat your bowl

Tomato Sauce
1 to 2 Tbsp extra-virgin cold pressed olive oil
1/2 organic yellow onion, diced small
1/4 cup organic carrots, diced small
2 garlic cloves, minced
2 tsp fresh thyme leaves, pick the leaves off
1 can (28-oz) whole peeled tomatoes (San
    Marzano brand gives the best flavor)
3 Tbsp extra-virgin cold pressed olive oil
Pinch of sea salt and fresh ground pepper

Toppings
1 cup fresh mozzarella, grated
1 cup Gruyere or Swiss cheese, grated
1 cup hard cheddar cheese, grated
2 tsp fresh rosemary, chopped fine

INSTRUCTIONS

Begin a few hours ahead, you will have breaks while waiting for your dough to rise. Start with the dough preparation: In large bowl, combine water, milk and yeast, stir gently with a fork to incorporate everything. Add the 2 cups flour, salt and olive oil. Mix only until it begins to form a very sticky, messy looking dough.

Lightly flour your work surface (1/4 cup to start) and move the dough to the work surface. Begin kneading by alternately folding it over and pushing it down, fold over again, push down, etc. Keep going until the dough is smooth and elastic, no longer sticky.

Rub the inside surface of a large bowl with some olive oil, place the entire dough inside the bowl. Cover with a clean dry kitchen towel, and put the bowl in a warm place to let the dough rise for 1 to 1 1/2 hours. It will expand to double or triple of its original size.

In the meantime, prepare your tomato sauce: In a medium pot, add olive oil. When hot, add the diced onions and carrots to "sweat" (extract flavors) for 2 to 3 minutes, until the onions are transparent. Add the garlic and thyme leaves, stir slowly for 1 minute.

Add the entire can of whole tomatoes by pouring all the liquid in and crushing the whole tomatoes with your hand before dropping into the pot. Make sure all the tomatoes are well crushed. Stir everything together and bring to a boil. Add a pinch of sea salt and black pepper. Stir and reduce to a simmer, then cover and simmer for 20 to 25 minutes.

Remove the tomato mixture from heat and pour

into a blender. Set aside the pot to use again.

Purée until all the vegetables are blended into a sauce consistency. Pour the sauce back into the pot, cover with the lid slightly ajar and set aside.

When your dough has risen properly, remove the towel and punch the dough in the bowl with your fist to let the air out. Turn the dough over, form it back into a ball and recover it in the bowl with the same towel. Again, let it rise in a warm place for 1 more hour.

Preheat oven to 425 degrees. Lightly oil a large baking sheet or pizza stone with 1 to 2 Tbsp olive oil. Set aside while you roll your dough.

Once your dough has risen for the second time, lightly flour your working surface again and put the dough onto the surface, flatten it slightly with your hands and begin working with a large

rolling pin. Roll it out into any shape you'd like, as long as its an even thickness throughout, approximately 1/2-inch thick. Carefully lift the edges of the dough and lay onto your baking sheet or pizza stone.

Spoon on the tomato sauce evenly, leaving a 1-inch margin at the edges of the pizza dough. Sprinkle the chopped rosemary, layer all the various cheeses and put into preheated oven to bake for 20 to 25 minutes or until the dough is lightly firm.

Remove the pizza with a wide flat spatula onto your cutting surface. Slice as you wish.
Serve the pizza hot with the Caesar Salad on the side.

Other options: Sprinkle a few red chili pepper flakes onto pizza. Feel free to substitute other types of cheese.

Pan-Toasted Quinoa with Marinated Kale Cranberry Salad

Serves 4

Carefully follow the instructions for making the quinoa and it will be the best you've ever had. My other secret in this recipe is marinating the kale overnight.

INGREDIENTS

Quinoa

    1 cup organic quinoa
    1 1/2 cups filtered water
    1 tsp garam masala
    1/2 tsp sea salt
    1/2 cup goji berries (aka wolfberries)
    2 tsp organic sesame oil
    1 stalk organic celery, diced
    1/2 yellow bell pepper, diced
    2 organic green onions, diced
    1/2 cup almonds, soaked overnight

Marinated Kale and Cranberry Salad

    1 bunch organic kale, washed, dried,
        sliced horizontally into 1/2-inch strips
    1/2 cup extra-virgin cold pressed olive oil
    1/2 cup dried, unsweetened cranberries
    1/2 cup pine nuts
    Juice of 2 organic lemons
    1/4 tsp cayenne powder (optional)
    Sea salt and fresh ground black pepper to taste

INSTRUCTIONS

For the Quinoa dish, soak the 1/2 cup almonds in filtered water overnight.

For the kale salad, put the sliced raw kale and

cranberries into a large serving bowl with the lemon juice and olive oil; toss well making sure that all the leaves are coated. Use a glass or ceramic bowl because the lemon juice will react with a metal bowl. Cover and marinate overnight in the refrigerator.

On the day of your meal, rinse and drain the almonds. If you would like to remove the outer almond skins, now is a good time. Roughly chop the drained almonds and set aside.

Remove the kale salad from the refrigerator and bring to room temperature.

In the meantime, toast the pine nuts in a dry pan over a medium heat until lightly golden. Add the toasted pine nuts to the salad and toss. Season to taste with sea salt, pepper and cayenne if you wish. Toss again and set aside for serving.

Rinse and drain the uncooked quinoa. Place a large pan on high heat, add the quinoa and pan toast until dry by using a wooden spoon to stir constantly until the grains are golden and dry, and all the moisture is gone.

In a small pot, add the filtered water, sea salt and garam masala. Bring to a boil, then remove from heat and pour into the pan with the pan-dried quinoa, stir together. Bring the quinoa and water mixture to a boil.

Add the goji berries and stir again. Reduce the heat to low and cover to simmer and cook. You want all the water to evaporate without letting the quinoa get too dry. This should take about 10 minutes but check as you get close to make sure the quinoa isn't over drying and sticking to the bottom of the pan. Remove from the heat and leave covered to finish cooking slowly. Set aside.

Heat a small skillet on medium heat, and when the pan is hot, add the sesame oil. Then add the diced celery, diced yellow pepper and sauté both until soft. Then add the green onions and sauté.

Remove from heat and pour this into the quinoa mixture. Sprinkle in the chopped almonds and using a large fork, very gently toss to "feather apart" the quinoa mixture so the individual grains separate into fluffy presentation.

Serve the Pan-Toasted Quinoa warm with the Kale Salad on the side.

Note: These dishes keep well in the refrigerator and are excellent as leftovers.

Chocolate Mousse

Serves 4

Chocolate mousse is French but I learned to make this mousse with whipped cream from a German chef. Our clients love it.

Note: you will need a large metal mixing bowl, one that can sit on top of a pot of boiling water.

INGREDIENTS

1 lb of 72% organic dark chocolate,
    chopped fine
4 organic free-range eggs
1 pint organic whipping cream

INSTRUCTIONS

Fill a large pot half-full with water and bring to a boil. In the meantime, put all your chopped chocolate in your large metal bowl. Set your eggs and whipping cream out on your counter. Place a medium size bowl next to your eggs, ready to use.

Once the water is rapidly boiling, place the large metal bowl with the chocolate on top of the pot of boiling water. It's important that the bottom of the bowl not touch the boiling water — you simply want to use the steam to melt the chocolate. Gently stir the chocolate at all times (to keep it from burning) with a heat resistant spatula. Once melted, remove the bowl from the steaming pot.

Into the medium bowl, crack all the eggs and beat thoroughly. The use of a hand mixer or blender is ideal but if you don't have one, use a wire whisk and whisk vigorously to whip the eggs to make the egg batter light and airy.

Into the large bowl of melted chocolate, slowly temper the eggs into the chocolate by gently using a whisk in one hand while simultaneously pouring (tempering) the eggs in with the other. If the eggs are added too fast, the eggs will scramble in the warm chocolate. Whisk slow and steady until everything is well incorporated. Set aside.

In another bowl, beat the whipping cream until you have stiff peaks, but don't overbeat or you will make butter! Gently fold the whipped cream into chocolate egg mixture. When well incorporated, pour into individual serving bowls, and refrigerate for at least 4 hours. Serve cold.

Other options: Sprinkle with slivered almonds if you'd like.

Chef
Licia Jaccard

Chef
Licia Jaccard

While born in the U.S., I grew up in France. My mother was French, from a traditional line of restaurateurs. She didn't want me to set foot in the business, deeming it too taxing for women. To appease her, I went to law school during the day and enrolled in Cordon Bleu's evening class program. I attended seminars and workshops with chefs and would convince them how desperate and determined I was to apprentice in their kitchens. That's how I spent vacations and free time.

After graduating from law school, I worked in the corporate world, at Yves Saint Laurent in Paris and then for varied U.S. corporations. I have always spent hours in the kitchen as a way to express my creativity, to solidify my relationships with friends and family and as an occasional source of therapy. Joan and I met on a recipe exchange website and went on to create a blog called the Cooking Light Critics, where we developed gourmet recipes along with others who did not want "bland" to be their lifelong diet.

In 2007 Joan told me that she and her husband, Oleg, were going to be part of an innovative new alcohol and drug treatment program and asked me to translate from French a book on a low-glycemic diet developed by Michel Montignac and to create recipes based on his healthy way of eating. I taught cooking to clients at the Malibu Beach Recovery Center for four years and I still provide desserts for special occasions, in part because Joan tells me alumni crave my desserts.

For me, cooking is a way of life, a way to experience ingredients at their source and transform them to fit specific needs. I love going to the market and thinking of recipes or ways of adapting recipes while I have the raw ingredients in my hands. I also think that to be able to cook and control what goes into your food is paramount to good health. For anyone, but more importantly for people with problems of all types (such as emotional eating, drug or alcohol abuse and anorexia), knowing what you put into your body is the first form of respect, where you can start taking care of yourself.

The cooking process is nurturing, caring, energizing and a great way to rediscover the body's proper functioning. Making things delicious and nutritious is an added bonus that solidifies your relationship with food. It is also a great source of creativity.

A few easy techniques will allow anyone to become their own personal chef. I love being the enabler of this learning experience, which has been the most rewarding aspect of my relationship with the Malibu Beach Recovery Center.

Breakfast
Lunch
Dinner
Dessert

Monday

Chef Licia Jaccard

Flat Zucchini Omelette

Serves 4

A great way to start the day is to eat a healthy breakfast in the morning. This omelette makes sure you have enough energy to start the day and is bulked up with zucchini to add extra flavor and crunch.

INGREDIENTS

1 lb small zucchini
   (reserve 8 zucchini slices for garnish)
1 3/4 tsp salt
2 Tbsp olive oil
1 tsp dried marjoram
8 large eggs
1 large pinch black pepper
1 Tbsp unsalted butter

INSTRUCTIONS

Trim ends of zucchini. Thinly slice 8 slices of zucchini and reserve for garnish. Coarsely grate all others on large holes of a box grater. Toss zucchini with 1 tsp salt in a large bowl and let stand 30 minutes.

Transfer zucchini to a colander and firmly squeeze handfuls to remove excess liquid.

Heat olive oil in a 10-inch heavy skillet over moderately high heat until hot but not smoking and sauté zucchini slices, stirring until golden. Reserve. Add grated zucchini to skillet and sauté in same olive oil 6 to 7 minutes. Remove skillet from heat and stir in marjoram, then let mixture cool to warm, about 15 minutes.

Lightly beat eggs with zucchini, pepper and remaining 3/4 tsp salt in a large bowl, using a fork.

Heat butter in a 7- to 8-inch nonstick skillet over moderately high heat until foam subsides and butter has a nutty fragrance. Add egg mixture, distributing zucchini evenly with a heatproof rubber spatula, and cook, lifting up egg around edges occasionally to let any uncooked egg flow underneath, until egg mixture is set around edge, about 1 minute.

Reduce heat to moderately low and cook omelette until softly set but top is still moist, about 3 minutes. Shake skillet to loosen omelette from pan, then slide omelette onto a large plate.

Wearing oven mittens, return omelette to skillet, browned side up. Cook omelette until underside is set, about 1 minute, then slide omelette onto a serving plate. Garnish with the reserved, browned zucchini slices.

Week Two / Licia Jaccard

Arugula, Pear and Roquefort Salad

Serves 4

This peppery leaf is tempered by the sweetness of the pears and the crunch of the pecans. The Roquefort adds an additional punch of flavor and a creaminess that makes this dish a refined go-to recipe for entertaining or an every day meal.

INGREDIENTS

1 lb arugula
2 ripe pears
3 oz pecans
3 oz Roquefort or blue cheese, crumbled
Vinaigrette
1/4 cup olive oil
3 tsp mustard
Juice of 1 lemon
Salt and pepper

INSTRUCTIONS

Peel and core the pears and cut in small thin slices. Mix together with the arugula, pecans and cheese. Whisk the vinaigrette ingredients and drizzle over plated salad at the very last minute.

Asparagus Chicken Stir Fry

Serves 4

Asian flavors really come alive in this dish. Do not be afraid of the heat in this dish, it can easily be tempered by serving it over a bed of basmati rice.

INGREDIENTS

> *1 tsp Thai red chile paste*
> *1 tsp fish sauce*
> *1 Tbsp black bean sauce*
> *1 Tbsp oyster sauce*
> *1/4 cup chicken stock*
> *16 oz chicken breast, cut into 1 inch pieces*
> *Whole-wheat pastry flour, as needed*
> *2 cloves garlic, minced*
> *1 chunk of ginger (about 1-inch thick), peeled and minced*
> *1 to 2 Serrano peppers, seeds removed and minced (WASH hands thoroughly)*
> *8 oz asparagus, trimmed and cut into 1 inch pieces (reserve tips)*
> *1 medium red bell pepper, seeded and sliced into pieces the same size*
> *2 scallions (green onions, spring onions), chopped into 1-inch pieces*
> *Sesame oil, to taste*
> *Peanut oil for deep-frying and stir-frying*

INSTRUCTIONS

Mix the red chile paste in with the fish sauce, black bean sauce, oyster sauce and chicken stock. Set aside.

Dredge chicken pieces in flour and deep fry in a small amount of peanut oil, remove when brown and set aside.

Put garlic, ginger and Serrano peppers in a clean wok with a small amount of peanut oil and cook until fragrant.

Add the asparagus pieces, saving tips for later. Stir fry and add the red pepper. Continue to stir fry, then add the chile paste, bean sauce and oyster sauce mixture. Add the cooked chicken and cook for about 1 minute, then add the reserved asparagus tips.

If desired, add 1 tsp whole-wheat pastry flour mixed in 1 tsp water to thicken mixture. Add the scallions, sprinkle with sesame oil and serve.

Broiled Salmon with Miso Glaze

Serves 4

This simple yet delicate dish is extremely quick to make. Purchase fresh salmon in season and serve it with grilled asparagus on the side. If you can get a larger portion of salmon, the leftovers are fantastic served cold with a simple salad.

INGREDIENTS

1 Tbsp sesame seeds
2 Tbsp sweet white miso paste
1 Tbsp reduced-sodium soy sauce or tamari
1 Tbsp minced fresh ginger
A few drops hot pepper sauce
1 1/4 pounds center-cut salmon fillet,
     cut into 4 portions
2 Tbsp thinly sliced scallions
2 Tbsp chopped fresh cilantro or parsley
Olive oil cooking spray

INSTRUCTIONS

Position oven rack in upper third of oven; preheat broiler. Line a small baking pan with foil. Coat foil with olive oil cooking spray.

Toast sesame seeds in a small dry skillet over low heat, stirring constantly, until fragrant, 3 to 5 minutes. Set aside.

Whisk miso, soy sauce (or tamari), ginger and hot pepper sauce in a small bowl until smooth.

Place salmon fillets, skin-side down, in the prepared pan. Brush generously with the miso mixture. Broil salmon, 3 to 4 inches from the heat source, until opaque in the center, 6 to 8 minutes.

Transfer the salmon to warmed plates and garnish with the reserved sesame seeds, scallions and cilantro or parsley.

Apple Crisp

Serves 12

This warm cobbler is the perfect ending to a long day. It reminds me of the flavors of baked apples in a more sophisticated way. The addition of old-fashioned oats in the topping gives it a very "country" feel that is filling yet refined. The apples can be replaced with a combination of fruits, including pears or peaches.

INGREDIENTS

2 to 2 1/2 pounds of sliced Granny
    Smith apples, fresh or frozen
1/3 cup agave syrup
1 1/2 tsp of lemon juice
1 1/2 tsp of whole-wheat pastry flour
1/2 tsp ground cinnamon

Topping

3/4 cup old-fashioned oats
1/4 cup agave syrup
1/2 cup whole-wheat pastry flour
1/3 tsp ground cinnamon
Dash of salt
1/2 cup of butter
1/2 cup of chopped walnuts

INSTRUCTIONS

Preheat oven to 400 degrees. Butter an 8x11 inch baking dish (use glass or stainless steel for best results).

Combine apples, agave syrup, lemon juice, flour and cinnamon in a bowl. Mix well to blend and transfer to the baking dish.

Mix old-fashioned oats, agave syrup, flour, cinnamon and salt in a large bowl. Add butter and rub into mixture until coarse crumbs form. Mix in walnuts. Spread topping onto apple mixture.

Place in the oven and bake until the topping is golden brown and the apples are tender, about 35 to 40 minutes.

Breakfast
Lunch
Dinner
Dessert

Tuesday

Chef Licia Jaccard

Gruyère Quiche

Serves 6

This is a staple dish at the Malibu Beach Recovery Center. The best quiche for breakfast, lunch with a salad, picnic or simple snack. Amazing, hot, cold or at room temperature. A definite winner.

INGREDIENTS

10 ripe tomatoes, halved and seeded
(or canned whole tomatoes, drain and halve)
Olive oil
1 tsp minced fresh garlic
1 tsp herbes de Provence
1 white onion, finely chopped
1/2 lb thick sliced turkey bacon or vegetarian
    bacon cut into 1/4 inch pieces
8 large eggs
2 cups crème fraîche or heavy whipping cream
1 Tbsp chopped fresh chives
1 cup shredded Gruyère cheese

INSTRUCTIONS

Preheat the oven to 300 degrees. Lightly grease a 10-inch round baking dish.

Arrange the tomato halves cut-side up on a baking sheet. Drizzle with olive oil, sprinkle with garlic, herbs and salt. Bake 1 1/2 to 2 hours. Set aside to cool. Do not turn off the oven.

Heat 1 Tbsp olive oil in a large skillet over medium heat. Add the onions and cook 3 to 5 minutes until softened but not browned. Transfer to a sieve to drain.

Add the turkey bacon to the skillet and cook over high heat, 5 to 7 minutes, until nicely browned. Drain on paper towel.

Break the eggs into a large bowl. Whisk in the crème fraîche. Stir in the chives, turkey bacon and onion.

Arrange the slow-roasted tomatoes in the baking dish and scatter the cheese over the top. Pour in egg mixture. The tomatoes will float to the top.

Bake 30 to 45 minutes until the top is golden brown and the custard shows no evidence of uncooked eggs.

Let cool slightly before cutting into wedges.

North-African Lamb Stew

Serves 6

Bring on the flavors of the Orient, the sweet and spicy mixtures of ingredients that make us want to travel far away and indulge in the romantic spell of the desert. Serve over couscous and let your inner Mata-Hari shine.

INGREDIENTS

3 Tbsp coriander seed
3 Tbsp cumin seed
3 Tbsp fennel seed
1 tsp hot red pepper flakes
Olive oil
2 1/2 lbs boneless leg of lamb or lamb shoulder, trimmed of any fat or gristle, cut into 2 1/4 in cubes
3 onions, sliced
1 Tbsp minced fresh ginger
1 tsp paprika
1/2 cup tomato purée
1/2 cup veal or beef stock
1/2 cup cooked chickpeas
1 1/2 lbs eggplant, cut into 1/4-in dice
4 large tomatoes
1 Tbsp chopped fresh cilantro
1/2 lb french beans, cut in 1" pieces
1 cup fresh or frozen peas
2 bay leaves

INSTRUCTIONS

Roast coriander seed, cumin seed, fennel seed and pepper flakes in a dry skillet over medium heat, stirring until fragrant, about 1 minute. Grind to a powder using a mortar and pestle or electric spice mill.

Season the lamb with salt. Heat 2 Tbsp olive oil in a large, heavy-bottomed saucepan over medium heat. Working in batches, cook the lamb, turning, until nicely browned on all sides. Drain the lamb in a colander placed over a bowl to catch the juices.

Add onions to the same pot, and cook until softened and golden in color 5 to 9 minutes. Transfer to the colander with the lamb. Finally, add the ginger to the pan and cook, stirring, just until fragrant, 1 to 2 minutes.

Turn the contents of the colander and the juice from the bowl beneath it back into the pan. Add the bay leaves, ground spices, paprika, salt to taste, tomato purée and stock. Bring to a boil. Add bay leaves, reduce heat to low and cook covered for 1 1/2 hours, or until meat is tender.

After one hour, while the meat is cooking, preheat the oven to 475°. Place the eggplant on a large baking sheet, drizzle with olive oil and sprinkle with salt. Roast 15 to 20 minutes or until golden brown.

To blanch the tomatoes, plunge into boiling water for 30 seconds to 1 minute, then place in ice water for another minute. Peel, quarter and remove the seeds, reserving the juice. Cut tomatoes into strips and reserve.

When the lamb is fork-tender, skim off any fat that has risen to the top. Pour tomato juices together with french beans and peas and cook for 10 minutes. Stir in the cooked chickpeas until heated.

Stir the cilantro into the stew and remove the bay leaves. Turn the stew into a shallow serving bowl. Scatter the eggplant and tomato strips over the top. Serve warm.

Bouillabaisse

Serves 6

A traditional French fish stew that has the streets of Marseille up in arms over who makes the most traditional recipe. This is a delight to make and to eat. Make sure you have enough friends around the table and bread to soak up the broth.

INGREDIENTS

Olive oil cooking spray
2 cloves garlic, minced
1 medium onion, chopped
*2 leeks, white part only, washed well and
    thinly sliced*
1/4 cup vegetable broth
3 medium tomatoes, seeded and chopped
1/2 Tbsp tomato paste
1/4 cup minced fresh flat-leaf parsley
2 sprigs fresh thyme or 2 tsp dried
2 bay leaves
1 piece (3-inch size) orange zest
1/4 tsp fennel seed
1/4 tsp saffron threads
1/8 tsp freshly ground pepper
*1/8 tsp crushed red pepper flakes or hot
    pepper sauce*
3 cups fish stock or bottled clam juice
Juice of 1 lemon
*1 pound lobster tails, meat removed and sliced
    into coins, shells reserved*
1/2 pound scallops
*1/2 pound jumbo shrimp, tail on, peeled and
    deveined*
*2 pounds any firm-fleshed fish, such as halibut,
    mahi-mahi, swordfish, grouper or red
    snapper, fillet and cut into l-inch strips*
8 whole-wheat crostini

INSTRUCTIONS

Coat a soup pot with cooking spray and add the garlic, onion and leeks. Sauté over medium heat for 5 minutes, stirring occasionally until soft. Add the vegetable broth, raise the heat and boil until the liquid has evaporated.

Lower the heat to medium and add the tomatoes, tomato paste, parsley, thyme, bay leaves, orange zest, fennel, saffron, ground pepper and red pepper flakes. Cook for 2 minutes.

Add the fish stock, 2 cups water and lemon juice along with the lobster shells. Bring to a simmer and cook for 15 minutes.

Remove the lobster shells, thyme sprigs and bay leaves from the broth. Remove the vegetables with a slotted spoon and purée in 4 batches with 1 cup of the broth in a blender or food processor until the soup is smooth.

Return to the pot and refrigerate until you are ready for dinner.

Just before you are ready to serve, bring the soup to a simmer. Add the lobster and cook for 2 minutes. Stir in the scallops and shrimp and cook for an additional 2 minutes. Add the fish and simmer, covered, until cooked through, another 3 minutes.

To serve, ladle the broth and seafood into shallow soup bowls. Top each serving with crostini.

Serve immediately.

French Chocolate Mousse

Serves 6

There is nothing to say except pure luxury and amazing indulgence. Sure this is not a calorie-free dessert, but the intensity of the chocolate taste and the richness of every bite will make this extraordinary dessert one of your favorites for entertaining and family gatherings. It is also said that chocolate is a mood enhancer.... hmmmm... pure pleasure.

INGREDIENTS

8 oz bittersweet chocolate, broken into pieces
2 tsp non-alcohol vanilla extract
8 Tbsp unsalted butter
8 large egg yolks
5 large egg whites

INSTRUCTIONS

Place chocolate, butter and vanilla in the top of a double boiler over simmering water. When chocolate has melted, stir until completely smooth.

Combine the egg yolks in a large bowl and beat until smooth. Mix in the chocolate while still lukewarm.

Place the egg whites in a large bowl and beat until stiff but not dry.

Add one third of the whites to the chocolate mixture and fold in to lighten. Pour the rest of the whites in the bowl and carefully combine with a spatula until no streaks of white are visible.

Pour into a serving dish and refrigerate for 2 hours or longer.

Breakfast
Lunch
Dinner
Dessert

Wednesday

Chef Licia Jaccard

Vegetable Frittata with Chèvre

Serves 4

This breakfast frittata was bulked up with vegetables and cheese, providing fiber, protein and dairy to your morning regime. This should keep you hunger-free until lunch and will make beautiful leftovers for snacks the next morning.

INGREDIENTS

2 medium zucchini, 1/4-inch dice
Salt and pepper
3 whole eggs plus 4 egg whites (7 total)
6 oz chèvre
1 Tbsp olive oil
1 Tbsp butter
4 scallions, thinly sliced
1/3 pound mushrooms, thinly sliced
1 yellow pepper, diced
1 red pepper, diced

INSTRUCTIONS

Preheat oven to 400 degrees.

Toss the zucchini in a colander with salt and place over a bowl, allow to drain for about 20 minutes. Squeeze out the liquid. Set aside.

Beat the eggs (whole and whites) in a medium bowl. Season with salt and pepper.

Heat the olive oil and butter in a 10-inch non-stick skillet and add the scallions, mushrooms, yellow pepper and red pepper. Sauté for about 4 minutes. Add the zucchini and stir to coat with the oil. Brown the zucchini slightly and then add salt and pepper to taste.

Add the egg mixture, lower the heat then add the cheese and cook until the mixture is almost set.

Place the skillet into the oven to finish cooking the frittata, about 5 to 7 minutes. Remove the skillet and loosen the edges with a spatula. Invert onto a serving platter and cut into wedges.

Balsamic Chicken with Caramelized Onions

Serves 4

This is a classic Italian recipe. I love the mixed flavors of the sweet caramelized onions with the tangy taste of the balsamic reduction. It gives the impression of a very complex dish when it is actually really easy and quick to make.

INGREDIENTS

2 large red onions
3 tsp chopped rosemary
1/2 tsp salt
1/2 tsp fresh ground pepper
4 (6-oz) skinless boneless chicken breast halves
1 1/2 Tbsp oil
1/4 cup balsamic vinegar
1/4 cup water

INSTRUCTIONS

Chop enough of the onions to equal 1/3 cup. Slice remaining onions and set aside.

Combine chopped onions, 2 tsp of rosemary, 1/4 tsp of the salt and 1/4 tsp of the pepper in a large zip-lock bag. Add the chicken. Squeeze out air and seal evenly. Refrigerate 20 minutes.

Meanwhile, melt the oil in a large non-stick skillet over medium heat and add the reserved sliced onions. Cook, stirring occasionally until softened and the onions begin to caramelize, about 12 minutes.

Add the vinegar, water and 1/4 tsp pepper. Bring to a simmer and cook, until liquid is almost evaporated and onions are very tender, 5 minutes.

Spray a ridged grill-pan with nonstick spray; heat pan over medium heat. Remove the chicken from the bag and discard the marinade. Grill chicken, turning occasionally, until cooked through, 10-12 minutes.

Serve with the onions.

Italian Pasta and Bean Soup with Sausage

Serves 4

This soup is satisfying on so many levels: it brings you warmth, coziness, incredible taste and a sensation of being completely satisfied. Welcome to Italy!

INGREDIENTS

31 oz canned white beans, small variety, drained and rinsed

2 sprays olive oil cooking spray

1 tsp olive oil

1/2 pound cooked chicken sausage, Italian-style, cut into bite-size pieces

1/8 oz fresh sage, about 3 to 4 medium leaves, finely chopped

2 medium garlic cloves, minced

28 oz canned crushed tomatoes, with puree

1 Tbsp canned tomato paste, or to taste

2 1/2 cups water

3 cups canned chicken broth

1 tsp table salt, or to taste

Pepper to taste

3 oz uncooked whole-wheat spaghetti, broken into small pieces

1/4 tsp red pepper flakes, or to taste

INSTRUCTIONS

Purée half of beans in a blender; set aside.

Coat bottom of a large soup pot with cooking spray, then add oil and heat over medium heat. Add sausage and cook stirring frequently, until sausage starts to brown, about 2 to 3 minutes. Add sage and garlic and cook, stirring constantly, until fragrant, about 1 minute.

Add puréed beans, whole beans, crushed tomatoes, tomato paste, water, broth, salt and pepper to pot. Bring soup to a boil, stir in spaghetti. Continue cooking soup according to time specified by pasta manufacturer.

Season to taste with salt and red pepper flakes. Yields 1 1/2 cups per serving.

Cherry-Almond Clafouti

Serves 6

Clafouti is a rustic, simple French dessert that's a cross between a pancake and custard. You can use other fruits according to season.

INGREDIENTS

1/2 cup whole almonds (about 2 ounces)
1 1/4 cups whole milk
1/2 cup agave syrup
8 oz dark sweet cherries, pitted, halved (about 2 cups)
3 large eggs, room temperature
1/2 tsp almond extract
Pinch of salt
1/4 cup whole-wheat pastry flour

INSTRUCTIONS

Blend almonds in processor until ground but not pasty. Transfer to small saucepan, add milk and bring to simmer. Remove from heat, let steep 30 minutes. Pour through fine strainer, pressing on solids to extract as much liquid as possible. Discard solids in strainer.

Preheat oven to 375 degrees. Butter a 10-inch-diameter glass pie dish. Scatter cherries evenly over bottom of dish.

Using electric mixer, beat eggs, almond extract, salt and agave syrup in medium bowl until well blended. Add strained almond milk and beat to blend. Sift flour into egg mixture and beat until smooth. Pour mixture over cherries.

Bake until set and knife inserted into center comes out clean, about 30 minutes. Cool completely.

Let stand at room temperature. Serve. (Can be made 6 hours ahead.)

Breakfast
Lunch
Dinner
Dessert

Thursday

Chef Licia Jaccard

Stone Fruit Salad with Toasted Almonds

Serves 6

An unexpected morning meal. The combination of fruit, cheese, nuts and greens makes it a satisfying, energizing and delicious meal.

INGREDIENTS

3 Tbsp lemon juice
1 Tbsp almond oil
1/4 tsp salt
1/8 tsp black pepper
8 cups mixed salad greens
3 plums, sliced
2 peaches, peeled and sliced
2 nectarines, peeled and sliced
2 apricots, peeled and sliced
3/4 cup pitted fresh cherries, halved
1/4 cup (2 oz) crumbled goat cheese
2 Tbsp sliced almonds, toasted

INSTRUCTIONS

Stir together lemon juice, vinegar, oil, salt, and pepper.

To serve salad, toss salad greens and fruit with dressing. Sprinkle with goat cheese and sliced almonds. Serve immediately.

Filet Mignon with Peppercorn Mustard Sauce

Serves 4

This is a classic rendition of a typical French dish. Serve it with sweet potato fries!

INGREDIENTS

- 1/4 tsp salt
- 1/4 tsp coarsely ground or cracked black pepper
- 4 (4-oz) beef tenderloin steaks (1 1/2 inches thick)
- 1 tsp olive oil
- 1/3 cup minced shallots
- 2/3 cup fat-free beef broth
- 1/4 cup green pepper corn mustard or Dijon mustard

INSTRUCTIONS

Sprinkle salt and pepper over steaks. Heat oil in a 9-inch cast iron skillet over medium high heat until hot. Add steaks. Cook 5 minutes on each side or until desired degree of doneness.

Remove steaks from skillet; keep warm. Add shallots to skillet; sauté 30 seconds. Add broth and mustard, stir well. Reduce heat, cook 2 minutes, stirring constantly. Serve steaks with sauce.

Week Two / Licia Jaccard

Asparagus, Peas and Basil Salad

Serves 6

A tender salad that lends itself to many interpretations.

INGREDIENTS

1/4 cup finely chopped shallots

3 Tbsp unsalted butter

2 lbs asparagus, trimmed and cut into
    1-inch pieces

3/4 lb shelled fresh peas (2 1/2 cups or
    1 3/4 pound in pods) or 1 (10-oz)
    package thawed frozen peas

1/2 tsp fine sea salt

Handful of torn basil leaves (about 3/4 cup)

INSTRUCTIONS

Cook shallots in butter in a 12-inch heavy skillet over medium heat stirring frequently, until just tender, about 4 minutes.

Stir in asparagus, peas, sea salt and 1/4 tsp pepper, then seal skillet with foil. Cook over medium heat until vegetables are tender but still slightly al dente, about 8 minutes.

Stir in basil and sea salt to taste.

Grilled Salmon with Lime-Butter Sauce

Serves 6

So easy to make, and yet, so delightful. Serve with green vegetables or a side of browned Brussels sprouts. The contrast makes it interesting and surprising.

INGREDIENTS

6 fillets of salmon, center-cut with skin still attached

Olive oil to coat grill

1 1/2 tsp finely grated lime zest

1 large garlic clove, chopped

1/4 cup fresh lime juice

1 tsp salt

1/2 tsp black pepper

1 stick (1/2 cup) unsalted butter, melted

INSTRUCTIONS

Heat grill and lightly spread a coat of oil. Grill flesh-side down, approximately 4 minutes. Turn fillets over, cover pan and grill until just cooked through, 4 to 6 minutes.

Purée garlic with lime juice, salt and pepper in a blender until smooth. With motor running, add melted butter and blend until emulsified, about 30 seconds.

Sprinkle fillets with lime zest and top each with 1 Tbsp of sauce. (Lime butter sauce can be made 1 day ahead and chilled, covered. Stir before using.)

Week Two / Licia Jaccard

Chocolate Decadence with Raspberry Coulis

Serves 12

This very simple cake has an almost brownie-like texture. It is dense, intense and gets a burst of flavor from the raspberry coulis that accompanies it.

INGREDIENTS

1 lb bittersweet chocolate,
   chopped into small pieces
10 Tbsp unsalted butter, room temperature
4 large eggs
1 Tbsp agave syrup
1 Tbsp whole-wheat pastry flour
(plus more for dusting baking pan)

Whipped Cream
1 cup heavy cream
1 tsp non-alcohol vanilla extract

Raspberry Coulis
2 lbs frozen raspberries,
   thawed and with juices
1/2 tsp lemon juice
4 Tbsp agave syrup

INSTRUCTIONS

Preheat oven to 425 degrees. Butter an 8 or 9 inch layer cake pan or spring form pan. Line bottom with parchment paper. Butter the paper and dust with flour.

Place chocolate and butter in top of double boiler over simmering heat. Once melted, stir and combine completely. Remove from heat.

Beat eggs and agave syrup until light and fluffy, about 5 to 10 minutes. Reduce to low speed and beat in flour. Fold in egg mixture to chocolate mixture. Pour into prepared pan.

Bake for exactly 15 minutes. Let cool completely to room temperature. Do not refrigerate. Invert onto serving platter and remove parchment paper.

Raspberry Coulis: Place raspberries, lemon juice and agave syrup in food processor and puree thoroughly. Pass through a sieve to remove seeds.

Whipped Cream: To whip cream, place cream in standing mixer and beat on high speed. Add in vanilla when cream is just coming together.

Serve chocolate cake with raspberry coulis and whipped cream.

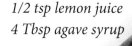

Breakfast
Lunch
Dinner
Dessert

Friday

Chef Licia Jaccard

Sourdough Grilled Cheese Sandwich

Serves 1 or 4 as a side to a salad

This comeback from childhood is all the comfort food you will ever want. A twist on the cooking process gives it a crisp and flavorful outside while the inside is pure melted goodness. Can be served with a cup of tomato soup on a chilly winter night.

INGREDIENTS

2 slices sourdough bread
2 oz shredded or thinly sliced Fontina cheese
2-4 Tbsp unsalted butter, softened
4 fresh sage leaves
1 Tbsp grated Parmigiano cheese

INSTRUCTIONS

Heat a non-stick skillet on medium-low to medium heat. Spread one side of bread with butter. Press two sage leaves on the butter, and brush the leaves with a little more butter so they adhere. Repeat with second slice of bread.

Lay one slice of bread in hot pan, butter and sage side down. Place cheese on the bread in the pan. Top with second slice of bread, butter and sage side up. Grill for a few minutes. You will hear the butter start to sizzle. Carefully check bottom of sandwich and cook until golden brown. With a spatula, carefully flip the sandwich, and cook for another few minutes, again until golden brown.

Sprinkle the top of the sandwich with half of the Parmigiano, making sure to cover the sage leaves. Flip the sandwich back over and cook for a few seconds to crisp the Parmigiano. Don't leave it too long or the Parmigiano will burn. Sprinkle the rest of the Parmigiano on the top slice and flip once more to crisp that side.

Remove immediately from pan and place on a plate to cool for a few minutes until ready to serve.

Steak with Chimichurri Marinade

Serves 4

Once again, a simple recipe that is easy to prepare and provides a spectacular taste that makes the individual ingredients shine. The steak can be grilled on a barbecue or grilled in a cast-iron pan with similar success.

INGREDIENTS

Chimichurri

1 1/2 cup Spanish olive oil
Juice of 2 limes
1 1/2 cup finely chopped fresh parsley
8 cloves garlic, finely chopped
2 shallots, minced
2 Tbsp each finely chopped fresh basil, thyme and oregano
Salt and pepper to taste

Gaucho Steak

2 lbs skirt steak, cut crosswise into 4 equal portions
Salt and pepper

INSTRUCTIONS

Combine the chimichurri ingredients in a bowl and season with salt and pepper. Divide between 2 bowls. Use half as the marinade and half as the dipping sauce.

Place the steak in a large baking dish and pour half of the chimichurri over it. Turn to coat, cover and marinate in the refrigerator for 2 hours.

Remove steak from the refrigerator and let it come to room temperature while preheating the grill to high. Remove it from the marinade and season with salt and pepper. Discard the marinade.

Grill the steak for 4 to 5 minutes on one side until browned, turn, and grill another 4 to 5 minutes for medium-rare. Remove from the grill, let the meat rest for 10 minutes.

Slice thinly on the bias. Serve with the remaining chimichurri on the side.

Twice-Baked Goat Cheese Soufflés

Serves 8

Great for entertaining, made ahead, they only need reheating when your guests arrive. Serve with a simple salad for an elegant appetizer.

INGREDIENTS

> 3 Tbsp butter plus more for coating ramekins
> 1 cup dry whole-wheat breadcrumbs
> 3 Tbsp whole-wheat pastry flour
> 1 cup milk
> 10 oz soft goat cheese
> 3 egg yolks
> Salt and pepper to taste
> 1 cup egg whites (about 7 large eggs)

INSTRUCTIONS

Position the rack in the center of the oven and preheat the oven to 425 degrees. Butter eight 5-ounce ramekins, making sure to coat them well. Coat each ramekin with breadcrumbs then turn them over and tap out the excess. Reserve any remaining breadcrumbs.

Melt the 3 Tbsp butter in a stainless-steel skillet over medium-high heat. Whisk in the flour and cook for 20 seconds. Whisk in the milk and cook for about 1 minute, whisking constantly, until the mixture has thickened to the consistency of a thin, pourable pudding.

Crumble 8 ounces of the goat cheese into a large mixing bowl. Pour the hot milk mixture over the goat cheese and mix well. Add the egg yolks and

mix again. Season with salt and pepper. Using an electric mixer with clean, dry beaters, beat the egg whites in a large bowl until stiff peaks form. Fold half of the whites into the cheese mixture to lighten it. Then gently fold in the remaining whites.

Divide half of the soufflé mixture among the prepared ramekins. Crumble the remaining 2 ounces of goat cheese and divide among the ramekins, then top with the remaining half of the soufflé mixture, dividing it equally among the ramekins. Sprinkle the remaining breadcrumbs over the top.

Place the ramekins in a large baking pan and pour in boiling water to come halfway up the sides of the ramekins. Bake for about 25 minutes or until the soufflés are golden. Remove from the oven and let stand, still in their water bath, for 15 minutes.

Using a towel to hold the ramekins, run a knife around the inside rim to loosen. Turn the soufflés out onto a baking sheet. The soufflés may be held at room temperature for up to 6 hours before the final baking.

When ready to serve, heat the soufflés in a 425 degree oven for 5 to 7 minutes, or until deep golden brown. Serve with a salad.

Grilled Shrimp Salad with Avocado, Mango and Peanut Dressing

Serves 2

*This simple yet beautiful salad represents so well our
Malibu Beach Recovery Diet that it is featured on the cover.
Classy, artful and elegant while rich in taste and in health benefits.*

INGREDIENTS

1 lb shrimp, peeled and deveined
1 Tbsp sesame oil
1 tsp red pepper flakes
1 lime, zested and juiced
2 Tbsp unsweetened coconut milk
1 Tbsp fish sauce
1 Tbsp peanut butter
1 jalapeno pepper, finely sliced
1 tsp coconut palm sugar
1 Tbsp cilantro, chopped
1 Tbsp mint, chopped
1 mango, peeled and sliced
1 avocado, peeled and sliced
2 handfuls of salad greens
2 green onions, sliced
2 Tbsp peanuts, roasted and chopped (optional)

INSTRUCTIONS

Place the shrimp in a bowl with the oil and red pepper flakes. Toss to ensure that the shrimp are evenly coated in the oil. If grilling on a barbeque, skewer the shrimp and cook 2 to 3 minutes on each side. If grilling in a pan, heat 1 tsp oil in a heavy pan and throw in the shrimp when the oil is about to start smoking. The shrimp will curl up and change color and be done when opaque throughout. Set aside to cool while making the salad dressing.

In a small bowl, zest and juice the lime and add the remaining seven ingredients (up to the chopped mint) and set aside.

Arrange the mango, avocado, salad greens, green onions and shrimp on a serving plate and sprinkle with the dressing. Serve garnished with roasted, chopped peanuts.

Butternut Squash Barley Risotto

Serves 4

Not all grains are created equal. This delicious and nourishing risotto makes a perfect substitution for Aborio rice

INGREDIENTS

2 Tbsp olive oil

1 butternut squash (medium, about 2 pounds), peeled, seeded and cut into 1/2-inch cubes (about 3 1/2 cups)

3/4 tsp salt

3/4 tsp ground black pepper

6 cups low sodium vegetable broth

1 cup water if necessary

4 Tbsp unsalted butter

2 small onions, chopped

2 medium garlic cloves, minced

2 cups pearl barley

1 1/2 oz grated Parmesan cheese

2 Tbsp minced fresh sage leaves

1/4 tsp fresh grated nutmeg

INSTRUCTIONS

Heat oil in a 12-inch nonstick skillet over medium-high heat until shimmering but not smoking. Add butternut squash in an even layer and cook without stirring until golden brown, 4 to 5 minutes. Stir in 1/4 tsp salt and 1/4 tsp pepper. Continue to cook, stirring occasionally, until squash is tender and browned, about 5 minutes longer. Transfer squash to bowl and set aside.

Return skillet to medium heat; deglaze with broth until all brown bits have dissolved. Transfer to a large saucepan, cover saucepan and bring mixture to simmer over high heat, then reduce heat to medium-low to maintain a simmer.

Melt 3 Tbsp butter in the now empty skillet over medium heat; when foaming subsides, add onions, garlic, remaining 1/2 tsp salt and pepper. Cook, stirring occasionally, until onions are softened, 4 to 5 minutes. Add barley to skillet and cook, stirring frequently, until grains are translucent around edges, about 3 minutes.

Add 1 1/2 cup broth and cook, stirring frequently, until fully absorbed, 4 to 5 minutes. When first addition of broth is fully absorbed, add 3 cups hot broth and half of reserved squash to barley. Simmer, stirring every 3 to 4 minutes, until liquid is absorbed and bottom of pan is almost dry, about 12 minutes.

Stir in about 1/2 cup hot broth and cook, stirring constantly, until absorbed, about 3 minutes, repeat with additional broth 2 or 3 more times, until barley is al dente. Take off heat, stir in remaining 1 Tbsp butter, Parmesan cheese, sage and nutmeg. Gently fold in remaining cooked squash. If desired, add up to 1/4 cup additional hot broth to loosen texture of barley risotto. Serve immediately.

Figs and Balsamic Syrup with Vanilla Ice Cream

Serves 4

This highly flavorful dessert is an immediate favorite. The balsamic reduction has a sweet caramel-like flavor that marries perfectly with the ice cream. For a healthier version, replace the ice cream with Greek yogurt.

INGREDIENTS

1/2 cup balsamic vinegar
1/2 cup orange juice
1 Tbsp agave syrup
1/2 tsp non-alcohol vanilla extract
2 cups black Mission figs, stems removed and
    cut in half vertically
1 cup heavy cream
1 tsp pure non-alcohol vanilla extract
2 pints vanilla ice cream with no sugar added

INSTRUCTIONS

Combine the vinegar, orange juice, agave syrup and vanilla in a small saucepan. Bring to a boil. Reduce the heat to medium-low and cook until the mixture is thick and syrupy, 12 to 15 minutes. Add the figs, turning to coat evenly, and cook for 1 minute. Remove from the heat and cool slightly.

Beat the cream in a medium bowl until soft peaks form. Add the vanilla and beat until stiff peaks form.

To assemble, place a small dollop of whipped cream in each of the 4 serving glasses. Add the ice cream and divide the figs evenly, reserving 4 halves for garnish. Top with whipped cream and garnish with the fig halves.

Breakfast
Lunch
Dinner
Dessert

Saturday

Orange French Toast

Serves 6

Crisp, not soggy — perfect for a large group since it is all ready at the same time! The subtle hint of orange makes this breakfast favorite remarkably light and healthy.

INGREDIENTS

2 cups of fresh orange juice
1 tsp of non-alcohol vanilla extract
2 cups half-and-half
1 tsp orange extract
6 eggs, beaten
2 (1 pound) loaves of day old whole-wheat
    French bread
1/2 cup agave syrup
1/2 cup (1 stick) unsalted butter
1 jar sugar-free orange marmalade

INSTRUCTIONS

Preheat oven to 325 degrees.

Mix first 5 ingredients together and pour into a large shallow dish. Cut French bread (diagonally) into 1 inch slices. Soak bread (2 minutes max) on each side.

Brown slices in butter over medium-low heat in large skillet. When all are browned, place on cookie sheets (in a single layer) and bake 20 minutes.

Remove from oven. Place on a serving dish and serve hot with agave syrup and sugar-free orange marmalade.

Curried Apple Couscous

Week Two / Licia Jaccard

Serves 4

An interesting mix of texture and flavor make this couscous anything but bland. Can be eaten as a side or as a main dish with a salad.

INGREDIENTS

4 Tbsp unsalted butter (divided)
1 Tbsp curry powder
1 medium apple, cored and chopped
3 green onions, washed, trimmed, thinly sliced
1 cup whole-wheat couscous
1 3/4 cup water
1 tsp sea salt
1/2 cup pine nuts, toasted
Small handful of mint, chopped

INSTRUCTIONS

In a large saucepan over medium-high heat, add 3 Tbsp butter, curry powder and a couple generous pinches of salt, cook for a minute or until the spices are fragrant. Stir in the chopped apples and cook for about 3 minutes, enough time for the apples to soften up a bit and absorb some of the curry. Scoop the apples from the pan and set aside in a separate bowl.

In the same pan, again over medium-high heat, add the remaining butter. Stir in the green onions, let them soften up a bit and then add the water and salt. Bring to a boil, stir in the couscous, cover and remove from heat. Steam for 5 to 10 minutes and then use a fork to fluff up the couscous. Stir in the apples, pine nuts and chopped mint.

Season with more salt and curry powder to taste.

Hot Garlic Shrimp and Asparagus

Serves 4

This dish will remind you of the Caribbean islands, with the heat of the peppers mixed in with the freshness of the shrimp. Can be made into an appetizer or finger foods for a party, the trick is to cook the shrimp just enough so that they are fully cooked and crisp without being rubbery.

INGREDIENTS

2 Tbsp olive oil
2 1/2 cups (1-inch) sliced asparagus (about 1 pound)
2 tsp minced garlic
1/2 tsp salt
1/4 tsp crushed red pepper
1/4 tsp freshly ground black pepper
1 1/2 pounds peeled and deveined large shrimp
2 Tbsp lemon juice
4 cups cooked basmati rice

INSTRUCTIONS

Heat oil in a large nonstick skillet over medium heat. Add asparagus, garlic, salt and peppers and cook for 2 minutes, stirring frequently. Add shrimp and cook for 4 minutes, stirring frequently, until the shrimp are no longer pink and have curled up.

Stir in lemon juice, bring to a boil. Remove from heat and serve over basmati rice.

Week Two / Licia Jaccard

Chicken Tortilla Soup

Serves 6

Do not let the list of ingredients deter you, this is one of the easiest soups to make. The flavors are layered for a maximum taste but the process is remarkably easy. Invite some friends over or take it to work the next day, this is a perfect crowd-pleaser.

INGREDIENTS

1 tsp olive oil
1 cup chopped onion
2 garlic cloves, minced
2 cups shredded cooked chicken breast (about 10-oz)
1/4 cup vegetable broth
1 Tbsp seeded, chopped jalapeño pepper
1 tsp ground cumin
1 tsp Worcestershire sauce
1/2 tsp chili powder
2 (14 1/4-oz) cans no-salt-added chicken broth
1 (14.5-oz) can diced peeled tomatoes, undrained
1 (10 3/4-oz) can condensed reduced-fat, reduced-sodium tomato soup (such as Campbell's Healthy Request), undiluted
1 1/4 cups crushed whole-wheat tortilla or pita wedges, toasted
1/2 cup fat-free sour cream

INSTRUCTIONS

Heat oil in a Dutch oven over medium-high heat. Add onion and garlic, sauté 2 minutes.

Stir in next 9 ingredients (chicken through tomato soup), bring to a boil.

Reduce heat and simmer for 1 hour. Ladle soup into bowls; top with tortilla or pita chips and sour cream.

Apple Galette

Serves 8 to 10

Serve this traditional Parisian dessert with vanilla ice cream, lightly sweetened whipped cream, or crème fraiche.

INGREDIENTS

Dough
  1 1/2 cups whole-wheat pastry flour
  1/2 tsp salt
  12 Tbsp cold unsalted butter, cut into
      1/2 inch cubes (1 1/2 sticks)
  7 to 9 Tbsp ice water

Apple Filling
  2 lbs apples (3-4 medium or 4-5 small)
  2 Tbsp unsalted butter, cut into
      1/4-inch pieces
  2 Tbsp sugar-free apricot preserves
  1 Tbsp water

INSTRUCTIONS

Combine flour and salt in food processor with three 1-second pulses. Scatter butter pieces over flour, pulse to cut butter into flour until butter pieces are size of large pebbles (about 1/2 inch), about six 1-second pulses.

Sprinkle 1 Tbsp water over mixture and pulse once quickly to combine; repeat, adding water 1 Tbsp at a time and pulsing, until dough begins to form small curds that hold together when pinched with fingers (dough should look crumbly and should not form a cohesive ball). Empty dough onto work surface and gather into rough rectangular mound about 12 inches long and 5 inches wide.

Starting at farthest end, use heel of hand to smear small amount of dough against counter, pushing firmly down and away from you, to create separate pile of dough (flattened pieces of dough should look shaggy). Continue process until all dough has been worked. Gather dough into rough 12 by 5-inch mound and repeat smearing process. Dough will not have to be smeared as much the second time and should form cohesive ball once entire portion is worked. Form dough into 4-inch square, wrap in plastic and refrigerate until cold and firm but still malleable, 30 minutes to 1 hour.

About 15 minutes before baking, adjust oven rack to middle position and preheat oven to 400 degrees.

Peel, core and halve the apples. Cut apple halves lengthwise into 1/8-inch-thick slices.

Place dough on a floured 16 by 12-inch piece of parchment paper and dust with more flour. Roll dough until it just overhangs all four sides of parchment and is about 1/8 inch thick, dusting top and bottom of dough and rolling pin with flour as needed to keep dough from sticking. Trim dough so edges are even with parchment paper. Roll up 1 inch of each edge and pinch firmly to create 1/2-inch-thick border. Transfer dough and parchment to rimmed baking sheet.

Starting in one corner, layer sliced apples to form even rows across bottom of dough, overlapping each slice by about one-half. Continue to layer apples in rows, overlapping each row by half. Dot apples with butter. Bake until bottom of tart is deep golden brown and apples have caramelized, 45 to 60 minutes.

While galette is cooking, combine apricot preserves and water in medium microwave-safe bowl. Microwave on medium power until mixture begins to bubble, about 1 minute.

Pass through fine-mesh strainer to remove any large apricot pieces. Brush baked galette with glaze and cool on a wire rack for 15 minutes.

Transfer to cutting board. Cut in half lengthwise and then crosswise into individual portions, serve.

Breakfast
Lunch
Dinner
Dessert

Sunday

Chef Licia Jaccard

Soft Scrambled Eggs with Mushrooms, Chives and Fleur de Sel

Serves 4

Forget the boring and rubbery scrambled eggs of days past, this elegant version will become one of your breakfast favorites.

INGREDIENTS

2 Tbsp unsalted butter
1/2 cup finely chopped mushrooms
4 Tbsp finely chopped fresh chives
8 eggs, lightly beaten
Fresh ground black pepper, to taste
Fleur de sel or other finishing salt, to taste

INSTRUCTIONS

Melt butter in a medium skillet. Sauté the mushrooms for 3 minutes, then add the chives and cook for another minute, until fragrant.

Add eggs and black pepper. Cook the eggs over very low heat, stirring constantly, until cooked to the desired doneness. Quickly add fleur de sel and scramble for just a few more seconds. Serve immediately.

Chicken Niçoise

Serves 6

You can add as many vegetables as you want to personalize this dish, but just as it is, it sings of the French countryside and summer scenery.

INGREDIENTS

1 whole chicken, about 5 lbs
4 onions
4 eggplants
2 green bell peppers
2 red bell peppers
5 zucchini
6 large ripe tomatoes
1/4 cup olive oil
1 bouquet garni (herb bouquet)
2 garlic cloves
1/4 cup pitted olives
Salt and pepper

INSTRUCTIONS

Cut the chicken along the joints and sauté in saucepan over high heat in olive oil. When meat turns golden brown, remove from pan and set aside.

Mince the onions and peppers and sauté in a saucepan over high heat in the remaining oil. When well browned, remove and then brown the sliced eggplant and zucchini. Return the onions and peppers to the pan, then the meat.

Scald the tomatoes for 30 seconds, then peel, seed and dice them. Add to the pan with the garlic, bouquet garni, salt and pepper. Cover and simmer over low heat for 1 hour. Remove the bouquet garni, add the olives and serve.

Barley Risotto with Dried Apricots and Hazelnuts

Serves 4

This is one of my favorite risottos and I love to have any leftovers for breakfast. The mix of sweet from the apricots and crunchy from the hazelnuts are a perfect compliment to the chewy grain. Another winning recipe.

INGREDIENTS

4 cups organic vegetable broth
2 cups coconut milk
3 Tbsp olive oil
1 medium onion, finely chopped
1 garlic clove, minced
1/4 tsp salt
1/4 tsp black pepper
1 1/4 cups pearl barley
1/2 pound dried apricots, chopped
1 1/4 tsp finely grated fresh lemon zest
1 ounce finely grated Parmigiano (about
   1/2 cup) plus additional for serving
1/2 cup hazelnuts, toasted and coarsely
   chopped

INSTRUCTIONS

Heat broth and coconut milk in a pan and cover.

In a 4-5-quart heavy pot over moderate heat, cook onion and garlic in olive oil with salt and pepper, stirring occasionally, until softened, about 5 to 7 minutes. Add barley and cook, stirring, 1 minute. Add 1/2 cup broth mixture and boil, stirring, until liquid is absorbed, about 1 minute.

Add 4 cups broth mixture and bring to a boil, covered, then reduce heat and simmer, covered, until barley is tender (it should be chewy) and mixture is thickened to a stew-like consistency, 35 to 40 minutes.

When barley is cooked, add in apricots and enough additional water to thin to desired consistency and cook over moderate heat, stirring, until hot, about 1 minute. Stir in lemon zest and cheese, then season with salt and pepper. Serve with hazelnuts and additional cheese on the side.

Week Two / Licia Jaccard

Grilled Sea Bass with Tapenade

Serves 4

The flavors of the Mediterranean have gotten to me once more. This rendition of a favorite recipe will bring sunshine to your plate.

INGREDIENTS

4 sea bass steaks, skin on, about 4 to 6 oz each
1 Tbsp each chopped, fresh chervil, basil and
    tarragon

Marinade
Juice of 1 lemon
3 garlic cloves, chopped
1 tsp ground coriander
1/4 cup olive oil

Tapenade
1 1/2 cup kalamata olives, pitted
2 Tbsp drained capers
4 flat anchovy filets, drained
3 garlic cloves
2 Tbsp chopped fresh parsley
Juice of 1/2 lemon
1/4 cup olive oil

INSTRUCTIONS

In a glass or ceramic dish, mix together the lemon juice, garlic, coriander and olive oil. Add fish steaks, turning to coat. Marinate covered in the refrigerator up to 2 hours.

To prepare the tapenade: In a food processor, combine the olives, capers, anchovies, garlic, parsley, lemon juice and olive oil. Process, pulsing the machine on and off, until a coarse paste forms. Transfer to a small bowl and refrigerate until needed.

Preheat the oven to 400 degrees. Remove fish from marinade and pat dry. Arrange sea bass steaks on an oiled baking sheet without crowding. Season lightly with salt. Bake until the fish is just cooked through, about 10 minutes.

Brush each piece of fish with 1 tsp of tapenade.

To serve, place a fish steak on each of 4 warmed serving plates and top with a spoonful of tapenade. Scatter herbs over the top and serve at once.

Mango Mousse

Serves 6

Another easy favorite to prepare ahead of entertaining. It is a visually beautiful dish that packs the flavors in a very healthy rendition of the traditional mousse.

INGREDIENTS

2 large ripe mangoes, peeled and seeded
3/4 cup yogurt
2 Tbsp frozen orange juice concentrate
2 egg whites
1 lime sliced thinly

INSTRUCTIONS

Purée mango, yogurt and orange juice concentrate in food processor.

Beat egg whites until stiff. Gently fold into the mango puree.

Pour into 6 glasses or ramekins and place in the freezer for 30 minutes.

Garnish each with the lime slices.

Week Two / Licia Jaccard

Chef
Johnnie Handal

Chef
Johnnie Handal

I'm a private chef who started working at Malibu Beach Recovery Center in April 2012. I love private cooking. I find it's more intimate than cooking in a restaurant. Everyone plays a part in healing the people who come here.

A few clients are a little rowdy and unhappy when they first join us. They hate everyone. But after a week or so of detoxing, attending process groups, doing yoga and following the diet, they start to get a natural glow about them. It's amazing to watch them undergo the healing process. Their mood changes, they're happier; they smile and laugh more often.

The kitchen is the center point of the house and where clients congregate. I overhear clients talking, relating that their addiction has been the number one priority in their lives. They probably couldn't have cared less about food. But after they've been here a few weeks, I notice that food has become important to them — learning about the diet or how to cook certain foods. Clients have asked me, "Do you mind if I learn how you're going to make that?" "Can I watch you?" "What are you doing there?"

That's great to hear. I love teaching people. Some clients learn to cook the meals on their own. I've had several people tell me they want to stay on the diet afterward. They believe it has helped them. And they like the food. Why shouldn't they? It's tasty. Before leaving, they want to know what they can make and if I will email them some of their favorite recipes. I've stayed in touch. After they leave, they can go out and eat anything they want. But the ones on the

right path stay on the diet. It's become ingrained in them that this is what's going to help them stay clean and sober.

I went to a French culinary school and grew up in my family's Italian restaurants, but I like to say I'm a multiethnic chef; there's no one type of food I prefer. I cook Chinese, South American, Asian….everything. I believe I can make anything healthy and low glycemic by a few simple substitutions and upping the flavor; healthy food doesn't have to taste like cardboard. I like to give clients a wide variety of cuisines, and I like to match the soup, salad and dessert to the ethnicity of the main course. If I'm making Jamaican food, for example, there's going to be a coconut or pineapple dessert.

If clients ask if they can ever cheat, I tell them, "You can't cheat when it comes to drugs to stay on track, so why would you cheat on the Malibu Beach Recovery Diet?"

Breakfast
Lunch
Dinner
Dessert

Monday

Chef Johnnie Handal

Italian Omelette

Serves 1

Herbs are a great way to add lots of flavor to anything. Basil, oregano, and garlic make this omelette not your typical morning breakfast, but a step above.

INGREDIENTS

3 eggs
Pinch of salt and pepper
1 small ripe vine tomato, diced
3 basil leaves
2 Tbsp Parmesan cheese, grated
2 tsp butter
1 tsp dry oregano
1 garlic clove, chopped finely

Special equipment: 6 to 8-inch nonstick aluminum sauté pan, rubber spatula

INSTRUCTIONS

Crack eggs into bowl, add salt and blend with fork.

Heat a 6 to 8-inch non-stick aluminum sauté pan over medium-high heat. Once pan is hot, add butter and garlic and brush around surface of pan.

Add tomato, basil, oregano and cook for about 2 minutes, stirring. Pour eggs into center of pan and stir with rubber spatula for 5-10 seconds. As soon as a semi-solid mass begins to form, lift pan and move around until the excess liquid pours off onto the sides of the pan. Using your spatula, move around the edge of the egg mixture to slide under the cooked omelette and loosen edge. Let omelette sit in pan for 10 seconds without touching. Add grated Parmesan to one half of the pan on top of the eggs.

Shake pan to loosen from pan. Lift up the far edge of the pan and snap it back toward you. Using your spatula, fold over half of the omelette. Slide omelette onto plate. Serve immediately.

Chicken Vegetable Soup

Serves 8

Soup can be a complete meal if you make it correctly. By using lean protein such as chicken and pairing it with lots of different vegetables, we get a one-dish meal that doesn't spike insulin.

INGREDIENTS

1 whole chicken, cut in 8 pieces, discard skin
1 small yellow onion, chopped 1/2 inch
6 garlic cloves, chopped
4 celery ribs, chopped
1/2 head cabbage, cut in squares
1 cup green beans, chopped
1/2 head cauliflower, chopped
1 8-oz can crushed tomatoes
2 Tbsp parsley, chopped
Salt and pepper

INSTRUCTIONS

Put chicken in a large soup pot and cover with water 2 inches above the chicken. Boil for 45 minutes. Take out chicken and let the chicken sit for 10 minutes to cool off.

Meanwhile add onion, garlic, celery, cabbage, green beans, cauliflower and canned tomatoes to the broth and cook for 15 minutes once the broth boils.

Pull the chicken off the bones and add back to the soup and let it all cook for 10 minutes.

Add parsley and taste the soup to add salt and pepper according to taste.

Grandma's Spaghetti and Meatballs

Serves 8

Low glycemic does not mean giving up pasta! By swapping out regular white pasta with low-glycemic or whole-wheat pasta, you can still enjoy grandma's spaghetti and meatballs.

INGREDIENTS

Sauce

- 1 lb spaghetti (preferred brand: Dreamfields - low GI)
- 2 28-oz cans San Marzano crushed roma tomatoes w/ juice
- 8 cloves garlic, chopped
- 2 Tbsp olive oil
- 8 basil leaves
- Salt to taste

Meatballs

- 2 lbs ground chuck 80/20
- 8 garlic cloves, chopped
- 3/4 cup chopped onion
- 1/2 cup Parmesan cheese, grated
- 2 eggs, beaten
- 2 slices whole-wheat bread, left out for a day
- 1/4 cup parsley, chopped
- 2 Tbsp milk
- 2 Tbsp dry oregano
- Salt and pepper
- 1/2 cup grated Parmesan cheese

INSTRUCTIONS

In a large sauce pot, heat olive oil and sauté garlic until lightly brown. Add canned tomatoes to pot.

In a large bowl, mix all the meatball ingredients together, keeping a light hand so as not to harden the texture. Scoop with an ice cream scooper and form balls 2 inches in diameter and place on a plate until all meatballs are ready. Make sure the tomato sauce is at a light simmer.

Delicately, place the meatballs into the tomato sauce. Cook on a low/medium heat so that the meatballs simmer and are completely submerged for 30 minutes. Chop basil and add to pot. After 5 minutes, taste sauce and add salt accordingly.

Place a large pot of salted water to boil. When water is at a rolling boil, add pasta and stir frequently with a wooden spoon. Watch time carefully to keep pasta at an al dente consistency. Drain pasta in a colander.

Place cooked pasta in a serving bowl and pour half of pasta sauce over pasta and mix well. Place meatballs around pasta. Pour remaining pasta over the middle and garnish with Parmesan.

Orange Olive Oil Cake

Serves 8

A nice, light dessert goes well with any meal. This airy cake gets its flavor from the zest of an orange and is easily sweetened without sugar.

INGREDIENTS

1/2 cup olive oil, plus extra for greasing pan
2 tsp orange zest orange, finely grated
1 1/2 cup whole-wheat flour
2 large eggs
1/3 cup agave syrup
1/3 cup coconut palm sugar
1/4 tsp kosher salt
1/2 tsp baking powder
1/2 tsp baking soda

Topping

1 cup berries
1 tsp orange zest
1/2 tsp non-alcohol vanilla extract
1 Tbsp agave syrup

Special equipment: 9-inch spring form pan or cake pan; lined on the bottom with parchment paper

INSTRUCTIONS

Position a rack in the middle of the oven and preheat to 350 degrees. Grease spring form pan with some oil, then line bottom with a round of parchment paper and oil the parchment paper.

Mix dry ingredients in one bowl and wet ingredients in another bowl. Combine both wet and dry ingredients and mix until smooth. Transfer batter to the spring form pan. Bake until puffed and golden, and a wooden toothpick inserted in the center of cake comes out clean, about 35 minutes.

Cool cake in pan on a rack for approximately 10 minutes, then run a thin knife around edge of pan and remove the side of the pan.

In a sauté pan, place the topping ingredients and cook for 5 minutes, then mash with a whisk. Transfer to a bowl and refrigerate while the cake is cooling.

Remove the bottom of the pan and peel off parchment, then transfer cake to a serving plate. When ready to serve, spoon topping on the cake. Serve additional topping in a separate bowl.

Breakfast
Lunch
Dinner
Dessert

Tuesday

Chef Johnnie Handal

Lemon Ricotta Pancakes

Serves 4

Pancakes are often made with white flour and drenched in sugary syrup. In this recipe, we've replaced those elements with low GI foods, and added creamy ricotta cheese and zesty lemon to satisfy your appetite.

INGREDIENTS

> 1 cup whole-wheat flour
> 1 Tbsp baking powder
> 1/2 tsp ground nutmeg
> 1/4 tsp salt
> 1 cup ricotta cheese
> 2 eggs
> 2/3 cup milk
> 1 Tbsp agave syrup
> 1 lemon, zested and juiced
> Butter, for griddle
> Agave syrup for serving

INSTRUCTIONS

Mix together the whole-wheat flour, baking powder, nutmeg and salt in a small bowl. Whisk together the cheese, eggs, milk, agave syrup, lemon juice and zest in a large bowl. Mix together the wet ingredients to the dry ingredients until they are smooth.

Place a griddle or nonstick large pan over medium high heat. Add a Tbsp of butter for each batch of pancakes.

Using a 1/4 cup measure, pour the batter onto the griddle for each pancake. Flip when bubbles form on the pancake. Cook on both sides until they are light golden brown.

Serve immediately with agave syrup.

Optional: Add blueberries to the agave syrup.

Moroccan-Spiced Chicken with Couscous

Serves 4

Couscous is a great substitute for rice and helps to keep the Glycemic Level low in this dish. Paprika, cinnamon and cumin lend some interesting flavors to this unique dish.

INGREDIENTS

Chicken

1 Tbsp olive oil
1 whole chicken, cut in 8 pieces
1 small yellow onion, sliced thin
1 tsp cumin
1/2 tsp ground coriander
1 tsp paprika
1 tsp cinnamon
4 cups chicken stock
2 Tbsp grated lemon zest
1 cup canned garbanzo beans, drained and rinsed
1 Tbsp agave syrup
1/2 cup green olives
Salt and pepper

Couscous

1 cup couscous
2 cups chicken stock
1 Tbsp unsalted butter
Salt and pepper
2 Tbsp parsley, freshly chopped

Special Equipment:
Dutch-oven, small pot

INSTRUCTIONS

Pat the chicken dry with paper towels and season with salt and pepper.

Heat a Dutch-oven over high heat and add the olive oil, onions and chicken. When the chicken is nicely browned, flip the pieces over to brown the other sides. Add the spices (cumin, coriander, paprika and cinnamon) to the chicken and stir to incorporate. Then add the chicken stock, lemon zest, garbanzo beans, agave syrup and the green olives and stir.

When the liquid is at a steady boil, cover loosely and bring to low simmer. Cook for 1 1/4 hours.

When there are 15 minutes left for the chicken to cook, start the couscous. Put the chicken stock and butter into a medium saucepan and bring to a boil over high heat. Add the couscous in one steady pour, stir once, cover with a tight-fitting lid and remove from the heat. Let sit for 5 minutes.

Fluff the couscous with a fork and place into a medium serving dish. Spoon the chicken pieces over the couscous and pour the remaining liquid into a separate bowl to serve on the side. Sprinkle the chicken with fresh parsley and serve.

Gumbo

Serves 8

Often okra is covered in white flour and fried but in this gumbo recipe we use fresh okra along with other hearty vegetables, and thicken with a roux made with whole-wheat flour and butter. It's flavorful and fills you up.

INGREDIENTS

2 Tbsp olive oil
6 cloves garlic, minced
2 cups onion, chopped
3/4 cup celery, chopped
1 cup bell pepper, chopped
12 oz okra, chopped
1/4 cup butter
1/4 cup whole-wheat flour
8 cups water
1 16 ounce can diced tomatoes
1 lb shrimp, deveined and shelled
1 lb boneless, skinless, chicken breasts, chopped
1 lb chicken sausage, sliced
2 bay leaves
1 pinch salt
1 tsp ground cayenne pepper
1 tsp ground black pepper
Gumbo file powder

INSTRUCTIONS

Melt butter in a large skillet over medium heat. Cook garlic, onions, celery, bell pepper and okra stirring constantly until golden brown. Set aside.

In a large heavy-bottomed stock pot over medium-high heat, combine butter and whole-wheat flour. Cook, stirring constantly, until the roux (which is an even mixture of butter and flour used to thicken sauces and soups) becomes brown. Stir in the vegetable mixture. Cook, stirring, until vegetables are tender. Stir in water and tomatoes. Add bay leaves, salt, cayenne pepper and black pepper. Bring to a boil, reduce heat, and simmer for 1 1/2 hours, stirring occasionally.

Add shrimp, chicken and chicken sausage to stock pot. Simmer an additional 10 minutes, stirring occasionally. Remove bay leaves, sprinkle with file powder, and serve.

Whole-Wheat Apple Fritters

Serves 8

This dessert gets most of its sweetness through the natural sugars in the apples, with a little help from coconut palm sugar rather than white sugar.

INGREDIENTS

2 cups whole-wheat flour
1/3 cup coconut palm sugar
1 1/4 Tbsp baking powder
1/2 tsp ground nutmeg
1 tsp salt
2 eggs
1 cup milk
2 quarts oil for deep frying
4 large apples, peeled, cored and diced
   into 1/2 inch pieces
Cinnamon Sugar for Dusting
1 tsp cinnamon
1/3 cup coconut palm sugar

INSTRUCTIONS

In a medium bowl, mix together flour, coconut palm sugar, baking powder, nutmeg and salt.

In a separate bowl, beat together eggs and milk. Stir milk mixture into flour mixture until smooth.

Heat oil to 375 degrees in a heavy bottomed deep pot or skillet. Mix apples into the batter and scoop with a 1/4 measuring cup and fry, a few at a time, for 2 minutes on each side turning once until golden.

Drain on paper towels and dust with cinnamon/coconut palm sugar mixture. Serve warm.

Breakfast

Lunch

Dinner

Dessert

Wednesday

Whole-Wheat French Toast

Serves 2

Nutmeg, cinnamon, agave…Oh my! How about French toast that has your mouth watering for more.

INGREDIENTS

3 eggs
2/3 cup milk
1 1/2 tsp non-alcohol vanilla extract
1/4 tsp ground nutmeg
1 Tbsp agave syrup
3/4 tsp cinnamon
6 slices whole-wheat bread
Canola oil spray

Special equipment: griddle pan

INSTRUCTIONS

Preheat griddle pan over medium heat, spray with canola oil spray.

Combine all ingredients, except for bread, in a mixing bowl. Dip the bread slices in the egg mix and flip over and dip. Cook until golden brown on both sides.

Serve with agave syrup.

Ropa Vieja

Serves 4

In a really great complete meal, you should have a nice balance of nutrition. This Cuban classic combines flank steak that offers protein, while the vegetables and array of herbs offer a great taste. To round off the meal, a side of basmati rice is a good choice.

INGREDIENTS

1 lb flank steak, trimmed
2 Tbsp olive oil
1 red bell pepper, sliced thin
1 green bell pepper, sliced thin
1 onion, sliced thin
1 celery rib, sliced thin
8 ounces whole canned tomatoes with juice,
    chopped
1 Tbsp tomato paste
3 garlic cloves, chopped
1 1/2 tsp ground cumin
1 tsp dried oregano
1 bay leaf
1 tsp salt
1/4 tsp black pepper
1/4 cup Spanish olives, cut in half

Yellow Rice

1 Tbsp olive oil
1 tsp cumin
1/4 tsp saffron threads, crumbled
1 cup basmati rice
2 cups water
3/4 tsp salt

INSTRUCTIONS

In a large pot, cook red and green peppers, onion and celery in olive oil over medium heat, stirring until cooked thoroughly and the onions are translucent. Add flank steak to pot, tomatoes with juice, tomato paste, garlic, cumin, oregano, bay leaf and salt and pepper; simmer uncovered for 1 1/2 hours.

Take tongs and pull apart flank steak and place back in stew. Stir in olives and simmer, uncovered, 5 minutes.

To make rice, in a heavy saucepan, heat the oil over moderately high heat until hot but not smoking and sauté cumin 30 seconds, or until it turns a few shades darker and is fragrant. Stir in saffron and rice and sauté, stirring, 1 to 2 minutes, or until rice is coated well. Stir in water and salt and boil rice uncovered for 15 minutes. Fluff rice with a fork. Serve Ropa Vieja on top of the yellow rice.

Jamaican Shrimp and Mango over Coconut Rice

Serves 6

When it comes to rice, white rice is very high on the glycemic index. By swapping it out for basmati, using unsweetened coconut milk, and using agave syrup instead of sugar, this is a recipe for success.

INGREDIENTS

2 lbs shrimp, peeled and deveined
2 Tbsp olive oil
1 red onion, sliced thin
1 Tbsp allspice
1/2 tsp cinnamon
2 mangos, skinned and thinly sliced
1 jalapeno, chopped
2 Tbsp white vinegar
2 limes, juiced
1/2 cup cilantro, chopped
1 Tbsp agave syrup

Coconut Rice
2 cups basmati rice
1 1/2 cup water
1 can unsweetened coconut milk
1 whole habanero

INSTRUCTIONS

In a medium pot add basmati rice, water, coconut milk, and whole habanero. Bring to a boil, reduce to simmer and cover for 15 minutes.

In a large sauté pan, add olive oil, red onion, allspice and cinnamon and cook for 5 minutes. Add mango, chopped jalapeno, white vinegar, lime juice and shrimp and cook for 3-5 minutes until shrimp is pink.

Add the cilantro and agave syrup and cook for 1 minute. Serve over coconut rice.

Pineapple Upside-Down Cake

Serves 8

The essence of allspice along with the natural sweetness in the pineapple makes this recipe a keeper.

INGREDIENTS

1 (8-oz) can sliced pineapple in pineapple juice
1/4 cup agave syrup
6 Tbsp butter, melted and divided in half
1 cup whole-wheat flour
1/4 cup coconut palm sugar
1 tsp baking powder
1/4 tsp salt
1/8 tsp ground allspice
1/8 tsp cinnamon
1/8 tsp cloves
2 eggs, lightly beaten
1/4 cup milk
1/4 cup pineapple juice

Special Equipment: 8-inch round baking pan

INSTRUCTIONS

Preheat oven to 350 degrees. Drain pineapple reserving 1/4 cup juice. Set aside.

In a small bowl, combine the agave syrup and 3 Tbsp melted butter. Stir until smooth. Pour into an ungreased 8-inch round baking pan. Arrange pineapple slices in a single layer on top.

In a small mixing bowl, combine whole-wheat flour, coconut palm sugar, baking powder, salt and spices. Add the eggs, milk, reserved pineapple juice and remaining butter. Beat just until combined. Pour over pineapple.

Bake for 30 minutes or until cake springs back when lightly touched. Cool for 5 minutes before inverting onto a serving plate. Serve warm.

Breakfast
Lunch
Dinner
Dessert

Thursday

Chef Johnnie Handal

Parfait with Homemade Granola and Berries

Serves 6

Sugar-free Greek yogurt is an excellent source of protein and is relatively low on the glycemic index. By making your own granola, you can control the content and leave out added sugars.

INGREDIENTS

Yogurt
   1 quart sugar-free plain Greek yogurt
   16 oz sliced fresh berries

Granola
   3 cups rolled oats
   1 3/4 cups almonds, finely chopped
   1/4 cup coconut palm sugar
   1/2 tsp dried ground ginger
   1 tsp ground nutmeg
   1 Tbsp ground cinnamon
   1/2 tsp kosher salt
   1/3 cup orange juice
   1/4 cup agave syrup
   3 Tbsp coconut oil

INSTRUCTIONS

Preheat the oven to 300 degrees.

In a large bowl, mix together oats, almonds, coconut palm sugar, ginger, nutmeg, cinnamon and salt.

In a saucepan, heat orange juice, agave syrup and coconut oil until warm and melted together.

Mix the wet ingredients into the dry ingredients until combined, then spread the granola evenly on a baking sheet. Bake for about 30 minutes, mixing it after 15 minutes, until the granola is deep golden brown. Remove from oven and cool.

To serve: In each of 6 bowls put 1 cup of yogurt, sprinkle with homemade granola, spoon 1/3 cup berries on top of each and serve.

Lobster Mac N' Cheese

Serves 4

This is a classic comfort food with a twist. Use a low-GI brand pasta and add extra protein with succulent lobster.

INGREDIENTS

1 1/2-lb lobster
1 lb rotini (Dreamfields)
2 cups whole milk
5 eggs
Salt and pepper
1 cup sharp Cheddar, shredded
1 cup Monterey Jack, shredded
1 cup American cheese, shredded

INSTRUCTIONS

In a large pot with 2 quarts boiling salted water place whole lobster and boil for 8 minutes. Drain and cool. Break shell and break the meat of the lobster into large chunks in a small bowl.

Preheat oven to 375 degrees.

Place a large pot of salted water to boil. When water is at a rolling boil, add pasta and stir frequently with a wooden spoon. Watch time carefully to keep pasta at an al dente consistency. Drain pasta in a colander.

In a bowl add milk, eggs, salt and pepper and mix well. Add the three cheeses and lobster meat. Add the pasta and mix well. Spoon into a 9x9-inch baking dish and bake for 40 minutes until the top forms a light brown crust. Serve hot.

Herb-Roasted Turkey Breast and Puréed Cinnamon Sweet Potatoes

Serves 8

Sweet potatoes are allowed because they digest differently than white potatoes (causing less of an insulin spike). They are a wonderful accompaniment to turkey, making this combination a holiday favorite.

INGREDIENTS

1 2-3 lb boneless turkey breast
2 Tbsp unsalted butter, melted
1 sprig rosemary, stem removed, chopped
4 sprigs thyme, stem removed, chopped
8 sage leaves, finely chopped
Salt, pepper and paprika

Sweet Potatoes
2 large sweet potatoes, peeled and diced
1/4 cup milk, warmed
2 Tbsp unsalted butter, sliced
2 Tbsp agave syrup
1 Tbsp ground cinnamon

INSTRUCTIONS

Preheat oven to 350 degrees. Place turkey breast on a roasting pan and place melted butter on top of turkey. Sprinkle chopped herbs and spices on top of turkey breast. Place in oven for 45 minutes or until internal temperature reaches 165 degrees.

In a large pan, add diced sweet potatoes and cover with water. Bring to a boil and cook for 20 minutes. Strain sweet potatoes and place in a blender with milk, butter, agave and cinnamon. Blend until smooth.

Serve sliced herb turkey breast with puréed cinnamon sweet potatoes.

Baked Apples with Walnuts

Serves 4

Agave syrup is a natural sweetener that replaces sugar. Sugar is high on the glycemic index causing a spike in insulin so we avoid it. Cinnamon, nutmeg and walnuts compliment the sweetness of the apples.

INGREDIENTS

4 Granny Smith apples
2 Tbsp agave syrup
2 Tbsp coconut palm sugar
4 tsp butter
1 tsp ground cinnamon
1 tsp ground nutmeg
1/4 cup chopped walnuts

INSTRUCTIONS

Preheat oven to 350 degrees.

Cut a slice off the bottom of the apple and scoop out seeds and stem. Place apples on baking dish cut side down. In a mixing bowl combine agave syrup, coconut palm sugar, cinnamon, nutmeg, agave syrup and walnuts. Place 1 tsp butter on top of each.

Bake in the oven for 40 minutes until the tops of the apples are golden brown. Serve hot.

Breakfast
Lunch
Dinner
Dessert

Friday

Chef Johnnie Handal

Whole-Wheat Biscuits and Chicken Sausage Gravy

Serves 4

Breakfast is the most important meal of the day. Start it with something this healthy and delicious. By using chicken sausage, and keeping the ingredients simple, this recipe is tasty and easy.

INGREDIENTS

Biscuits

    1 3/4 cups whole-wheat flour
    1 1/2 tsp baking powder
    1/2 tsp baking soda
    1 tsp salt
    6 Tbsp cold unsalted butter, cubed
    3/4 cup milk
    2 Tbsp melted butter

Gravy

    3 Tbsp olive oil
    1 1/2 lb chicken sausage, sliced 1/2 inch thick
    Salt and freshly ground pepper
    3 Tbsp whole-wheat flour
    2 cups whole milk

INSTRUCTIONS

Preheat the oven to 425 degrees.

In a bowl, whisk the flour, baking powder, baking soda and salt. Using a mixer, cut-in the butter until the mixture resembles coarse meal. Stir in the milk just until a dough forms.

Knead the dough on a cutting board just until it comes together. Roll out the dough 1/2 inch thick. Cut out 6, 2-inch rounds. Place the biscuits on a baking sheet and brush the tops with melted butter. Bake for 20 minutes, until the biscuits have risen.

In a large pan, heat the oil. Add the sliced chicken sausage; cook over high heat, turning the sliced sausage, until browned, 5 minutes. Mix in 1/2 tsp each of salt and pepper and whole-wheat flour; cook for 1 to 2 minutes. Add the milk and simmer, stirring, until thick, about 5 minutes.

Split the biscuits, top with gravy and chicken sausage and serve.

Asian Minced Chicken Lettuce Cups

Serves 4

When dealing with a low-glycemic diet, a good choice is always vegetables. With this dish, you fill up on vegetables and proteins, rather than sugars and fats.

INGREDIENTS

Sauce

1/2 cup low sodium soy sauce
2 Tbsp rice vinegar
1 Tbsp garlic, minced
1 Tbsp ginger, peeled and minced
1 tsp chopped fresh cilantro
1 tsp sesame seeds
1 Tbsp sesame oil

Filling

6 Tbsp olive oil
1 lb boneless, skinless chicken breasts, chopped fine
1/4 cup celery, diced
1/3 cup red bell pepper, diced
1/3 cup sugar snap peas, diced
1/3 cup white onion, diced
1 Tbsp ginger, peeled and minced
1 Tbsp garlic, minced
1/3 cup bean sprouts
1/2 cup mushrooms, sliced
2 Tbsp scallions, chopped finely
2 Tbsp pine nuts
Kosher salt
Butter lettuce, for serving

INSTRUCTIONS

In a bowl mix all ingredients for the sauce and set aside.

Remove the core from the butter lettuce, rinse leaves and pat dry with paper towel.

In a large skillet, heat olive oil over high heat. Add the chicken and cook for 3 minutes. Add all the vegetables and cook until chicken and vegetables are cooked through. Add the prepared sauce and cook for 3 minutes stirring frequently.

Fill the butter lettuce leaves with cooked mixture and garnish with scallions and pine nuts. Serve hot.

Baked Salmon over Sautéed Broccolini

Serves 4

Salmon is an excellent source of omega-3 fatty acids that compliment any diet. Citrus from the lemon always pairs well with fish.

INGREDIENTS

> 1 lb salmon filet
> 2 Tbsp olive oil
> 1 whole lemon, sliced
> 2 Tbsp parsley, chopped
> Salt and pepper

Broccolini

> 2 bunches broccolini
> 1 Tbsp olive oil
> 2 garlic cloves, chopped
> Salt and pepper
> 1/2 cup chicken stock

INSTRUCTIONS

Preheat oven to 400 degrees. Place salmon on a greased baking sheet. Drizzle with olive oil, salt and pepper. Place slices of lemon on top along with chopped parsley and bake for 15 minutes.

In a skillet place olive oil and garlic. Sauté on medium high and add whole broccolini and cook for 3 minutes. Add salt, pepper and chicken stock and simmer for 3 minutes.

Place broccolini on plate and serve salmon on top. Discard lemon slices from salmon.

Sweet Potato Pie with Whipped Cream

Serves 6

A pie doesn't have to be an enemy. In this delicious sweet potato pie, a homemade crust allows this recipe to ditch the white flour, and white sugar, making it a low-glycemic dessert.

INGREDIENTS

Crust
   1 1/4 cup whole-wheat flour
   1 stick cold butter, cubed
   1/4 tsp salt
   1 Tbsp coconut palm sugar
   4 Tbsp ice water

Filling
   3 Tbsp butter, melted
   1/3 cup coconut palm sugar
   2 Tbsp agave syrup
   1/2 tsp cinnamon
   1/4 tsp ground ginger
   1/8 tsp allspice
   1/4 tsp salt
   3 eggs
   2 cups mashed sweet potato
   1 cup milk

Whipped Cream
   1 cup whipping cream
   1 tsp non-alcohol vanilla extract
   1 Tbsp agave syrup

INSTRUCTIONS

For the crust: Place flour, butter and salt in a food processor. Pulse until the mixture resembles coarse meal. Add ice water and mix until combined. Remove and place on floured cutting board and knead a few times. Shape dough in the form of a disk, wrap in plastic wrap and place in the refrigerator for 1 hour.

Preheat oven to 350 degrees. In a large bowl, mix all the filling ingredients until smooth.

Roll the dough into a circle a few inches larger than your pie plate and line the pie plate with the dough. Cut the hanging edges of the dough and pinch the dough with your fingers to make a pattern on the outer rim of the dough.

For the filling: Mix all the ingredients together. Fill the pie crust with the sweet potato mixture and bake in the center of the oven for one hour. Remove and let cool for one hour.

For the whipped cream: In a mixer, whip together the whipping cream, vanilla and agave syrup until the cream forms stiff peaks.

Serve the cooled pie and present the whipping cream in a separate bowl.

Breakfast
Lunch
Dinner
Dessert

Saturday

Chef Johnnie Handal

Spinach and Cheddar Cheese Frittata

Serves 2

Who doesn't love cheese? In this dish, it is paired with yummy greens, and protein packed eggs.

INGREDIENTS

2 Tbsp olive oil
1 cup fresh spinach, torn
2 Tbsp sliced green onions
1 tsp crushed garlic
Salt and pepper to taste
6 eggs
1/3 cup heavy cream
1/2 cup Cheddar cheese, shredded

Special Equipment: Medium non-stick oven-proof skillet

INSTRUCTIONS

Preheat oven to 350 degrees.

Heat olive oil in skillet over medium heat. Mix in spinach, green onions, and garlic. Season with salt and pepper. Cook for 1 to 2 minutes, until spinach is wilted.

In a medium bowl, beat together eggs and heavy cream. Pour into the skillet over the vegetables. Sprinkle with Cheddar cheese and mix once. Place pan in the oven for 10-15 minutes until the egg mixture doesn't jiggle.

Remove from the oven and turn frittata out of the pan and onto a serving plate with the help of a rubber spatula. Serve immediately.

Chicken Cashew and Brown Rice

Serves 4

Take-out from Chinese restaurants can be laden with sodium and msg. By using low sodium soy sauce and chicken broth, we can control our nutrients. Cashews and egg add extra protein, while the majority of the remaining ingredients are fresh, yummy vegetables.

INGREDIENTS

2 cups brown rice
3 Tbsp low-sodium soy sauce, divided
1 egg white
1 lb boneless, skinless chicken, sliced thin
1 Tbsp sesame oil
1/2 cup low-sodium chicken broth
1 Tbsp agave syrup
2 Tbsp olive oil, divided
3/4 cup onion, chopped in 1/2-inch pieces
3/4 cup celery, chopped in 1/2-inch pieces
1/2 cup red bell pepper, chopped in 1/2-inch
2 Tbsp ginger, minced
2 garlic cloves, minced
3 green onions, chopped finely
1/2 cup roasted cashews

INSTRUCTIONS

In a medium pot make 2 cups of brown rice according to the package directions.

Combine 1 Tbsp soy sauce, egg white and chicken in a large bowl; toss well to coat.

Combine remaining 2 Tbsp soy sauce, sesame oil, broth and agave syrup in a small bowl.

Heat 1 Tbsp olive oil in a large nonstick skillet over medium-high heat. Add chicken mixture to pan; sauté 3-5 minutes. Remove from pan.

Heat remaining 1 Tbsp olive oil in the same pan as the chicken. Add onion, celery and bell pepper; sauté 2 minutes. Add ginger and garlic; sauté 1 minute. Return chicken mixture to pan; sauté 1 minute.

Stir in broth mixture. Bring to a boil; cook 2-3 minutes, stirring constantly. Add green onions and cashews and cook for 1 minute. Serve over brown rice.

Stuffed Peppers with Ground Turkey

Serves 4

Using a bell pepper in place of a tortilla, and a flavorful tomato sauce, ground turkey is an excellent way to be healthy and full at the same time.

INGREDIENTS

1 lb ground turkey
3 Tbsp butter
1 yellow onion, chopped
1 tsp chili powder
Salt and pepper
1 tsp garlic powder
1/2 cup basmati rice, rinsed
28 oz can tomato sauce, organic
    reserve 1/4 cup for later
4 green bell peppers
1 Tbsp parsley, chopped, for garnish

INSTRUCTIONS

Preheat oven to 325 degrees.

Brown the onion in butter. Add ground turkey to the pan, along with chili powder, salt, pepper and garlic powder. When meat is partially browned add rice and tomato sauce and mix well.

Cut tops off of green bell peppers. Remove seeds and ribs and fill with mixture. Place peppers in a baking dish. Top off each pepper with 1 T of the remaining tomato sauce. Cover with a lid or foil and bake for 1 1/2 hours.

Chunky Chocolate Chip Cookies

Yields 16 cookies

Chocolate doesn't have to be a diet disaster. Dark chocolate has a lot of health benefits. Besides the antioxidants it lends to food, 72% chocolate has less sugar and more flavor making these cookies delicious.

INGREDIENTS

- 1 cup (2 sticks) cold butter, cut into cubes
- 3/4 cup coconut palm sugar
- 1/4 cup agave syrup
- 2 large eggs
- 1 tsp non-alcohol vanilla
- 2 3/4 cups whole-wheat flour
- 1 tsp baking soda
- 1 tsp kosher salt
- 12 ounces 72% dark chocolate chips

INSTRUCTIONS

Preheat oven to 350 degrees.

In large mixing bowl of an electrical mixer and add butter, coconut palm sugar and agave syrup and mix until smooth.

Add eggs (one at a time), then vanilla and continue to mix.

In a separate bowl mix whole-wheat flour, baking soda, baking powder and salt. Add to wet ingredients and mix until combined. Add dark chocolate chips and mix only a few turns until combined.

Scoop the dough with your hands into balls about 1 1/2 to 2-inches round and place on greased cookie sheet.

Bake for 14 minutes.

Breakfast
Lunch
Dinner
Dessert

Sunday

Chef Johnnie Handal

Whole-Wheat Oatmeal Blueberry Pancakes

Serves 4

Blueberries in your oatmeal are always a fulfilling way to start off your day, but turning it into pancakes...will start your day off even better.

INGREDIENTS

1 1/4 cup whole-wheat flour
1 Tbsp agave syrup
2 Tbsp baking powder
3/4 tsp salt
1 1/2 cups dry oatmeal
1 1/4 cups milk
3 eggs, beaten
2 Tbsp butter, melted
1/2 cup fresh blueberries
2 Tbsp butter, for cooking

INSTRUCTIONS

In a large bowl, mix all ingredients but blueberries. Continue mixing until smooth. Gently fold in blueberries.

Pour batter about 1/4 cup at a time onto the heated, buttered pan or flat griddle. Cook 1 to 2 minutes, until bubbles form. Flip, and continue cooking until lightly browned.

Citrus Chicken Fajitas with Guacamole

Serves 6

Mexican food can be made healthy. By eliminating the traditional tortillas made with white flour, this recipe is meant to be served as a fajita plate. The citrus and vinegar lend tons of flavor to the chicken and vegetables, so you don't even need a tortilla. Top it with homemade guacamole and this meal won't disappoint.

INGREDIENTS

1 1/2 lb boneless, skinless, chicken breast
        sliced thin

Marinade

1 cup orange juice
1/2 cup safflower oil
1/4 cup lime juice
1/4 cup red wine vinegar
1 garlic clove, minced
1 Tbsp each of kosher salt, black pepper,
        cumin, chili and garlic powder

Fajitas

1 Tbsp olive oil
1 yellow onion, sliced thin
1 green bell pepper, sliced thin

Guacamole

3 ripe avocados
2 vine ripe tomatoes, diced
1/2 small red onion, diced
1 lemon, juiced
1/4 cup cilantro, chopped
1 small jalapeno, seeded
        and chopped
Salt and pepper

INSTRUCTIONS

In a large bowl mix together the marinade ingredients. Make sure the dry seasonings are completely incorporated into the marinade. Add meat to marinade and mix well. Cover bowl and place in refrigerator for 6-24 hours.

Remove chicken from refrigerator. Drain meat and pat dry. Heat olive oil in a sauté pan. Sauté onions and bell pepper for 5 minutes until soft and translucent. Add chicken to pan and cook for an additional 5 to 8 minutes until meat is cooked.

Scoop out the avocados and place in a medium bowl with tomato, red onion, lemon juice, cilantro, jalapeno, salt and pepper. Mash with a fork until smooth.

Serve guacamole with the meat, spreading the onions, bell pepper and pan juices around the meat.

Barbecued Tri-Tip with Homemade Pineapple BBQ Sauce

Serves 6

The Dijon mustard and chili powder give this sauce a kick and the lemon balances the flavors while also giving an extra antioxidant boost.

INGREDIENTS

Tri-Tip
1 tri-tip steak (2 to 3 lb), trimmed
2 Tbsp olive oil
Salt and pepper to taste

BBQ Sauce
1 cup tomato sauce, canned and with no sugar
1/2 cup pineapple juice, canned with no added sugar
3 Tbsp Dijon mustard
2 Tbsp Worcestershire sauce
3 Tbsp agave syrup
1 Tbsp lemon juice
2 tsp chili powder

Vegetables
1 bunch asparagus
Other vegetables of your choice

INSTRUCTIONS

Preheat BBQ grill on high.

In a saucepan mix together tomato sauce, pineapple juice, Dijon mustard, Worcestershire, agave syrup, lemon juice and chili powder, bring to a boil and reduce for 15 minutes until thickened.

Season tri-tip with salt and pepper and smear with olive oil. Prepare the vegetables for grilling, drizzle with olive oil and season with salt and pepper.

When the grill is hot, place the meat on the grill for 10 minutes on each side, closing the grill to cook the center on both sides. After 20 minutes touch the tri-tip to see how well cooked the center is. The tri-tip should be as tender as the palm of your hand. Cook longer to desired preference. Remove the meat with tongs, taking care not to pierce so the juices do not escape. Cover for 10 minutes with foil to let rest.

While the tri-tip is resting, place vegetables on the grill and cook until slightly charred.

Remove the foil and place the meat on a cutting board. Slice the meat against the grain in 1/4 – inch slices and serve with pineapple BBQ sauce, surrounded by grilled vegetables.

Mixed Berry Crumble

Serves 6

Mixed berries lend tons of flavor and not a lot of calories.

INGREDIENTS

1/2 cup whole-wheat flour (for crumble)
1/3 cup coconut palm sugar
1/2 tsp ground cinnamon
1 pinch salt
1/2 cup whole-grain rolled oats
4 Tbsp cold butter, cut into small pieces
6 cups mixed berries
2 Tbsp agave syrup
Juice of 1 lemon
2 Tbsp whole-wheat flour (for berries)

Equipment: 6-7 oz ramekins

INSTRUCTIONS

Preheat oven to 350 degrees.

In a bowl combine whole-wheat flour, coconut palm sugar, cinnamon, salt and rolled oats. Using a food processor, or your hands, cut in butter until crumbles form.

In a bowl, combine the berries with the agave syrup, lemon juice and whole-wheat flour and toss to coat. Pour into a baking dish. Top with crumble topping. Bake about 35 minutes. Serve warm.

Chef
Sergio Galvao

Chef
Sergio Galvao

G rowing up in Brazil, my mother loved to cook and I'd help her in meal preparation or decorating cakes for her home-based small catering business. I didn't plan to become a chef then, and pursued a career in the TV and film industry, but later in life I helped a chef produce a cookbook by researching recipes, shopping for ingredients and helping style the photos of the dishes. My love for good food, my childhood experience and the cookbook project sparked my interest in cooking professionally, so I enrolled in a culinary school in Sao Paulo, Brazil, that was a partnership between the Culinary Institute of America (CIA) and a hotel management program. All teachers came from the CIA in Hyde Park, New York.

From the nutrition classes, I learned to produce meals that were delicious, light on the body and packed with the essential nutrients that promote good health and well-being. I began to work as a personal chef and observed the response of my clients to the foods I served. I discovered that a meal could have an important role in mood swings and either make people more energetic and happier or heavy and moody. I started cooking meals that combined the best nutrition with the best gastronomic experience.

I began my career in the world of recovery from addiction and alcoholism at a sober living house here in Malibu. Aware of the relationship between diet and the recovery of the clients, I did my best to cook the healthiest way possible. But it was not until working at Malibu Beach Recovery Center that I really learned how to do it in a scientific way.

Initially I found it a bit challenging to cut high-

glycemic ingredients out of my cooking and had to exercise creativity to substitute with low-glycemic foods. After a short time I adapted all my recipes and could easily see the results as I watched the clients' progress in their recovery. To help change someone's lifestyle is extremely rewarding. As a chef, my pleasure is to please people and when they enjoy what I've made, that makes me happy. But seeing how I can help people overcome addiction or disease with a certain style of cooking is now the most important thing I can accomplish as a chef. Because in the end, it's about helping people turn their lives around.

Clients addicted to heroin, for example, come to us in very bad shape — unhealthy and physically intoxicated, their digestive system is a mess. But eating according to the Malibu Beach Recovery Diet changes them in just a few days. It calms them down and begins to restore their health. I believe that the meals we serve allow them to get through detox more quickly and act as a shortcut in their long recovery process. Working for Malibu Beach Recovery Center changed my way of cooking and seeing food. I always believed food is the best medicine and then I saw our patients get well every day in front of my eyes.

Breakfast
Lunch
Dinner
Dessert

Monday

Chef Sergio Galvao

Breakfast Burrito

Serves 4

Nice way to start the day. Satisfying, wholesome and healthy. Clients love it at the Malibu Beach Recovery Center.

INGREDIENTS

- 3/4 pound ground turkey meat
- 4 Tbsp olive oil, divided
- Salt and pepper
- 1 Tbsp chili powder
- Pinch of cayenne
- 1 large green pepper, large dice (1 inch squares)
- 1 large red pepper, large dice (1 inch squares)
- 1 red onion, large dice
- 5 eggs (organic brown eggs, if possible) slightly beaten
- 4 large whole-wheat tortillas
- 1/2 cup fresh cilantro, chopped
- 1 cup shredded mozzarella or pepper jack cheese
- Olive oil spray

INSTRUCTIONS

In a large skillet, heat 3 Tbsp of the oil and brown ground turkey meat, leaving it chunky. Season with salt and pepper, chili powder and pinch of cayenne. Remove meat from skillet when browned.

In the same pan, add 1 Tbsp more oil, sauté peppers and onion until softened, 3 or 4 minutes. Add the eggs to vegetables and cook until almost fully cooked. Remove from heat. Add browned meat to eggs mixture.

Put one quarter of the eggs-sausage mixture and one quarter of the cheese in each tortilla. Sprinkle chopped cilantro on top. Roll it like a cigar, folding ends to close burrito.

Heat a large nonstick skillet; spray some olive oil and grill burritos on both sides, 2 at a time, until brown.

Serve immediately, with store bought green or red salsa, if desired. If not serving immediately, transfer to baking sheet and heat in the oven for 5 minutes, covered with foil.

Spicy Mexican Hot Chocolate

Serves 4

The spices in this beverage warm up your body and kick start digestion. And it's so delicious!

INGREDIENTS

4 cups milk (almond, low-fat, soy or rice,
    according to preference)
4 Tbsp unsweetened cocoa powder
4 pinches cayenne pepper
1/2 cup agave syrup
1 tsp ground cinnamon

INSTRUCTIONS

Mix all the ingredients in a saucepan and heat until the liquid almost reaches the boiling point. Whisk the chocolate until foamy and serve right away in four large mugs.

Chicken Lasagna

Serves 6

Rich in calories, it's even richer in nutrition. Good way to disguise veggies for picky eaters. I serve it for lunch so people have time to burn calories throughout the day. Don't over indulge.

INGREDIENTS

3 Tbsp extra-virgin olive oil, divided
1 lb boneless skinless chicken thighs
1 large onion, chopped
1 green pepper, chopped
3 cloves garlic, minced
1 Tbsp ground fennel seeds
1 cup sliced mushrooms
3 cups canned diced tomatoes
2 cups chicken stock
2 cups spinach leaves
1/2 cup coarsely chopped basil leaves
1 cup ricotta cheese
1 cup shredded mozzarella
3/4 cup grated Parmesan cheese
12 large Dreamfields lasagna sheets
1/2 cup whole-wheat panko breadcrumbs
Béchamel
3 cups milk (low-fat, soy, rice or almond)
2 Tbsp butter
3 Tbsp whole-wheat flour
1 pinch freshly ground nutmeg
Salt and pepper

INSTRUCTIONS

Prepare the chicken sauce: Pat the chicken dry. Season it with salt and pepper. In a large pan, heat 2 Tbsp olive oil and sauté the chicken in batches, until brown on both sides. Remove the chicken from the pan and set aside.

In the same pan, add 1 Tbsp olive oil and sauté the chopped onions, peppers, garlic and fennel seeds for 2 minutes. Add the mushrooms and sauté 2 more minutes.

Return the chicken to the pan, add the tomatoes and chicken stock, and bring to a boil. Lower the heat and simmer for 40 minutes, until the chicken is very tender. With 2 forks, break the chicken in smaller pieces without shredding it too much. Add the spinach and basil leaves and allow the warm sauce to wilt in it. Adjust salt and pepper seasonings if necessary.

While the chicken cooks, cook the pasta al dente and make the béchamel.

Preheat oven to 400 degrees.

For the béchamel: Melt the butter in a saucepan, add the flour and cook it for 2 minutes, stirring the mixture continuously. Add the cold milk, whisking strongly to dissolve any lumps. Season with nutmeg, salt and pepper, cooking until the mixture is thickened enough to coat the back of a spoon (nappe), but still runny and liquid.

In a medium-size baking dish, pour a little of the béchamel in the bottom to coat it. Make a layer with 3 of the lasagna noodles, 1/3 of the chicken sauce with vegetables, 1/3 of cheeses, a bit of béchamel. Repeat process for 2 more layers. Cover the lasagna with the 3 last lasagna sheets, cover with béchamel, Parmesan cheese and panko bread crumbs. Bake it for 40 minutes, until bubbly and golden brown on top. Rest the lasagna for 25 minutes before serving.

Greek salad

Serves 4

Perfect companion for rich dishes. Enzymes in raw vegetables help the digestion of fats.

INGREDIENTS

1 cup cherry tomatoes, halved

1 cup cucumber, partially peeled, diced large, without seeds

1 yellow pepper, diced same size as cucumber

1/2 cup Kalamata olives, pitted and halved

1/4 cup lemon juice

2 Tbsp Dijon mustard

1/3 cup extra-virgin olive oil

2 Tbsp fresh oregano, coarsely chopped

1/2 cup fresh feta cheese

INSTRUCTIONS

Mix all the vegetables in a bowl. Whisk the lemon juice, mustard, olive oil and fresh oregano until emulsified in a medium-sized bowl.

Toss the vegetables with the vinaigrette and season with salt and pepper, according to taste and to saltiness of the feta. Let the salad marinate for 30 minutes.

Divide salad on 4 plates, straining excess vinaigrette. Sprinkle feta cheese on top.

Pecan-Crusted Salmon Fillet with Mashed Roasted Yams and Creamy Sautéed Collard Greens

Serves 4

It's an elegant meal that you can easily share with guests. I always serve lighter proteins at night. I believe we should go big on breakfast, a little lighter on lunch and much lighter for dinner.

INGREDIENTS

Fish

> 4 boneless skinless central cut 4 oz salmon
> fillets
> 6 Tbsp salted butter, at room temperature
> 3 Tbsp chopped parsley
> 3/4 cup chopped pecan nuts
> 1/2 cup whole-wheat panko breadcrumbs
> Juice of 1 lemon

Yams

> 1 pound yams, peeled and cut in large chunks
> 2 cloves garlic, finely minced
> 2 Tbsp olive oil
> 1 Tbsp smoked paprika
> 2 Tbsp chopped Italian parsley
> 2 Tbsp butter

Greens

> 2 bunches collard greens, washed, stemmed,
> chiffonade (stack leaves on top of each
> other, roll it like a cigar tightly and with a
> sharp knive, cut it really thin)
> 2 cloves garlic, finely minced
> 1 Tbsp olive oil
> 1 cup chicken or vegetable stock
> 1/2 cup heavy cream

INSTRUCTIONS

Preheat the oven to 400 degrees.

Prepare the fish: Pat the fish dry with paper towels and season both sides with salt and pepper. Mix the butter with the parsley, pecan nuts, panko, lemon juice and season with pepper to taste. Cover the top side of the fish with a 1/2 inch layer of pecan butter, pressing down to stick to the fish. Put the fillets on a baking sheet sprayed with olive oil and place in the refrigerator until it is time to bake.

Cook the yams: Toss the yams with olive oil, garlic, paprika, salt and pepper and bake at 400 degrees until soft when pierced with a paring knife. Transfer to a bowl and while still hot, add the butter and parsley and mash the yams with a wooden spoon until chunky but creamy. Cover with foil and keep warm in a 200 degrees oven until serving.

Bake the fish for 12 minutes in a 425 degree oven, or until the fish is fully cooked and lightly brown on top. Let the fish rest for 5 to 10 minutes before serving.

Make the greens: Sauté the collard greens with the garlic in a large skillet with the olive oil. Add the chicken stock and cook until the stock has almost evaporated. Add the heavy cream, salt and pepper to taste and cook until the sauce is thickened and coats the greens.

Spoon the yams onto four plates, cover with the collard greens and place the fish on top. Serve immediately.

Grilled Fruits with Orange-Cinnamon Reduction and Vanilla Ice Cream

Serves 4

Nothing can be more delicious and better for you than grilled fruit. Simple and nice way to finish a meal.

INGREDIENTS

- 4 slices pineapple (1 inch thick, cored)
- 4 apricots, pitted and halved
- 4 peaches, pitted and halved
- 1 1/2 cups orange juice from fresh oranges
- 1 Tbsp orange zest
- 1 tsp ground cinnamon
- 2 Tbsp fresh mint chiffonade (stack leaves on top of each other, roll it like a cigar tightly and with a sharp knive, cut it really thin)
- Vanilla ice cream with no sugar added

INSTRUCTIONS

Preheat oven to 400 degrees. Heat the grill of the barbeque to hot, or a cast iron pan with ridges on the stovetop.

Brush the fruits with oil and grill them until grill marks appear. Cut the pineapple slices in 4 pieces each and the peaches and apricots in half. Transfer the fruits to a baking dish.

Place the orange juice in a heavy saucepan and boil until the liquid is reduced to 1/2 cup. Add the orange zest and cinnamon and pour over the fruit. Bake for 10 minutes.

Scoop ice cream into 4 individual bowls. Spoon fruit slices over the ice cream and garnish with the mint chiffonade. Serve immediately.

Breakfast
Lunch
Dinner
Dessert

Tuesday

Chef Sergio Galvao

Eggs Cocotte

Serves 4

Easy and delicious way to start the day. Just the right amount of carbs and proteins. Always a hit when I serve it.

INGREDIENTS

4 eggs
3 cups tomato sauce (if store-bought, make
    sure it contains no sugar)
1/2 cup basil leaves, chiffonade (stack leaves
    on top of each other,
    roll it like a cigar tightly and with
    a sharp knive, cut it really thin)
1 cup heavy cream
4 Tbsp grated Parmesan cheese
4 slices of sourdough bread

INSTRUCTIONS

Preheat oven to 400 degrees.

Split the tomato sauce between 4 individual ramekins. Add 1/4 of the basil to each ramekin. Break 1 egg in each ramekin. Season each egg with salt and pepper. Pour 1/4 cup of cream over each egg. Sprinkle with Parmesan cheese. Transfer ramekins to a baking sheet.

On another baking sheet, put the 4 slices of bread. Brush with olive oil and sprinkle with Parmesan cheese. Put both baking sheets in the oven for 12 minutes.

Serve each ramekin with one slice of toast.

Strawberry Milk

Serves 4

Brings back memories of my childhood. Cold or hot, always fun.

INGREDIENTS

4 cups strawberries, cleaned and chopped
2 Tbsp non-alcohol vanilla extract
4 cups milk (low-fat, soy, almond or rice)
1/2 cup agave syrup

INSTRUCTIONS

Sauté the strawberries in a heavy saucepan with vanilla. Cook for 10 minutes.

Purée the strawberries in a blender; strain them in a fine sieve. Put the strained purée back in the blender with the milk and agave syrup. Mix well.

Serve hot or cold.

Mexican Fiesta

***Always a smashing hit with our clients!
Fun, delicious and nutritious.***

Serves 6

INGREDIENTS

Brown rice

 1 Tbsp olive oil

 1 garlic clove, minced

 3/4 cup long grain brown rice
  (basmati, if possible)

 1 1/2 cup chicken or vegetable stock

 3/4 cup tomato sauce

 3/4 cup chopped onion

 1 small red pepper, finely chopped

 1 1/2 tsp chili powder

 1 tsp cumin

 1 Tbsp kosher salt

Beans

 2 Tbsp olive oil

 1/2 large onion chopped

 2 garlic cloves, finely minced

 2 tsp cumin

 1/2 cup chicken or beef stock

 1 bay leaf

 1 Tbsp balsamic vinegar (surprise
  non-traditional secret ingredient)

 1 large can organic low-sodium black beans
  (drained from excess liquid but not rinsed)

Spicy Chicken

 Olive oil

 1 lb skinless and boneless chicken thighs

 Salt and pepper

 1/2 onion chopped

 2 garlic cloves, finely minced

 2 cups diced tomatoes

 1 cup chicken stock

 1 green pepper chopped

 1 Tbsp chili powder

 1 canned chipotle pepper finely chopped with 1
  tsp adobo sauce

 1/2 cup clean chopped cilantro

 1/2 cup green onions, cut into thin rings, white
  and green parts

Guacamole

 2 large avocados, ripe

 Juice of 1 large lemon

 1/2 cup finely chopped red onion

 2 Tbsp chopped cilantro

 Hot pepper sauce and salt to taste

 1 tomato, seeded and diced small

Salsa

 3 tomatoes, seeded and diced

 1/3 cup green pepper, diced small

 1/3 cup red onion, chopped

 1/8 cup tomato puree

 Juice 1/2 lemon

 2 Tbsp chopped cilantro

 Hot pepper sauce to taste

Slaw

 1/3 small green cabbage, finely sliced in
  mandolin

 1 medium carrot, grated large or julienne in
  mandolin

 1/4 cup white vinegar

 Salt to taste

Other

 8 whole-wheat tortillas

 Shredded Mexican cheese
  (serve on the side in a bowl)

INSTRUCTIONS

Make the brown rice: Heat the oil in a large saucepan. Add onion, garlic and rice. Sauté for a couple of minutes. Add all the other ingredients and bring to a boil. Cover the pan with a tight-fitting lid and lower the heat to simmer. Cook for 35 minutes; take off the heat and rest the rice for 15 or 20 minutes before fluffing it with a fork and serving it.

Cook the beans: In a saucepan, heat the olive oil. Sauté the onions for 2 minutes; add the garlic and the cumin and cook 2 more minutes. Add the stock, bay leaf, balsamic vinegar and beans, and season with salt and pepper. Cook for 20 minutes, partially covered, or until beans are very tender and broth is thickened.

Make the salsa: Mix all the ingredients in a bowl; season with salt and marinate for at least 30 minutes before serving.

For the slaw: Mix all the ingredients in a bowl. Marinate for 30 minutes.

Prepare the chicken: Season the chicken with salt and pepper. Brown it in olive oil in a Dutch oven in batches. Remove the chicken from pan and reserve. In the same pan, sauté the onions and garlic until softened. Add the chicken back to the pan, with the tomatoes, stock, peppers, chili powder and chipotle. Cook for 45 minutes, until the chicken is very tender. Adjust salt, if necessary. Using 2 forks, break the chicken into smaller pieces. Add half of the cilantro and half of the green onions and mix well. Use the other half of the herbs to garnish chicken.

Make the guacamole: Cut the avocados in half, remove the pit and scoop the pulp into a medium bowl. Add the lemon juice, red onion, cilantro, red sauce and salt. Smash into a chunky purée. Transfer the guacamole to serving bowl and garnish with diced tomato. Refrigerate until ready to use.

When everything is ready to serve, grill 8 small whole-wheat tortillas and wrap them in foil. Serve all dishes together family style.

Crab Cake Salad

Serves 4

Again, a lighter meat at night. And so delicious. Packed with goodness.

INGREDIENTS

Crab cakes

> 3/4 pound crab meat (lump), well drained
> 2 slices whole-wheat-bread, crust removed,
>   ground in food processor
> 3/4 cup mayonnaise
> Juice of 1 lemon
> 2 Tbsp chopped parsley
> 1 cup panko whole-wheat breadcrumbs
> Olive oil for sautéing

Sauce

> 1/2 cup mayonnaise
> 1/2 cup sour cream
> 2 canned chipotle peppers
> 1 tsp adobo sauce from the can of chipotle
>   peppers
> 2 Tbsp capers
> Juice and zest of 1/2 lemon
> 1/2 cup parsley leaves, loosely packed
> Salt to taste

Salad

> 4 handfuls of mixed greens
> 4 large heirloom tomatoes, cut into wedges
> 1/2 English cucumber, cut into thin rounds or
>   sticks
> 1/2 cup radishes, thinly sliced with a
>   mandoline

Orange vinaigrette

> 1/3 cup orange juice
> 2 Tbsp white vinegar or rice vinegar
> 1 Tbsp grated orange zest
> 2 Tbsp Dijon mustard
> 1/4 cup extra-virgin olive oil
> Salt and pepper to taste

INSTRUCTIONS

For the crab cakes: Mix all the ingredients, except for the panko breadcrumbs, in a medium bowl. Add salt and pepper to taste. Shape four crab cakes and coat them on both sides with panko. In a large pan, heat the olive oil just before the smoking point. Sauté the crab cakes until golden brown on the first side. Flip them just once with a spatula and, when brown on the second side, transfer to a baking sheet, cover in foil and keep warm in a 200 degree oven.

For the sauce: Mix all ingredients in a food processor until well combined and smooth.

For the orange vinaigrette: Mix all ingredients together in a metal bowl with a whisk, until emulsified.

For the salad: Put all ingredients together in a bowl. Toss the salad with just enough vinaigrette to coat the vegetables.

To serve, split salad onto 4 plates, top with a hot crab cake and top each cake with a generous dollop of sauce. Serve immediately.

Strawberry Shortcake

Serves 4

After a light meal, a little bit of richness. Clients simply love it!

INGREDIENTS

Garnish
 3 cups strawberries, washed and quartered
 4 Tbsp orange juice
 3 Tbsp agave syrup

Cake
 2 cups whole-wheat pastry flour
 2 tsp baking powder
 1/4 tsp baking soda
 2 Tbsp coconut palm sugar
 3/4 tsp salt
 1 cup heavy cream
 1/2 cup melted butter

Whipped cream
 1 cup heavy cream
 3 Tbsp agave syrup
 1 tsp non-alcohol vanilla extract
 1 tsp freshly grated orange zest
 1 pinch cinnamon
 Mint for garnish

INSTRUCTIONS

Preheat oven to 400 degrees.

Prepare the garnish: Toss all ingredients together in a small bowl and let the mixture sit in the refrigerator for at least 30 minutes.

For the cake: Mix all the dry ingredients in a bowl. Add the cream and butter and mix just until absorbed. Pour the batter into an 8-inch greased square pan. Place into the preheated oven for 18 to 20 minutes, until the top becomes light brown. Take the cake out and cool on a rack.

Make the whipped cream: Chill the heavy cream and mixer bowl in the refrigerator for 30 minutes or in the freezer for 5 minutes. Whip the cream with the wire whisk of the mixer until soft peaks form. Add the rest of the ingredients and mix until incorporated.

To serve: Either cut cake with a 4-inch diameter ring into 4 individual round portions or remove cake from pan, remove 1/2-inch outer crust and cut in four squares. Cut cakes horizontally in half.

On four individual plates, pour 1 Tbsp of the strawberry liquid; place the bottom half of the cake; moisten with a bit more of the liquid. Then spoon the whipped cream and half of strawberries. Top each cake with the top layer of the cake. Again, moisten with some of the strawberry liquid, add a generous amount of whipped cream and top with the rest of strawberries. Garnish with mint sprigs. Serve immediately.

Breakfast

Lunch

Dinner

Dessert

Wednesday

Chef Sergio Galvao

Breakfast Couscous

Serves 4

A bit unusual, replaces oatmeal beautifully. Rich in good carbs. A gentle way to treat your digestive system. Comforting, tasty, exquisite!

INGREDIENTS

3/4 cup whole-wheat couscous
1 cup coconut milk
1/2 cup milk (low-fat rice or almond)
1 Tbsp curry powder
1/3 cup dried apricots, cut in slivers
1/3 cup unsweetened dried cranberries
1/4 cup toasted pine nuts
1/4 cup agave syrup
1 tsp cinnamon

INSTRUCTIONS

Boil 1 cup water in a small pan. Pour couscous at once, turn off heat and leave it to sit for 5 minutes.

Meanwhile, bring coconut milk and other milk to a boil with curry powder and agave syrup.

To serve, fluff couscous with a fork; split into 4 individual bowls. Split dried fruits into bowl over couscous; pour milk in and sprinkle pine nuts and cinnamon on the top. Serve immediately.

Chai Tea

Serves 4

On the same note, calming and digestive. Overall a good breakfast after a dinner party where you might have overindulged in heavy foods.

INGREDIENTS

3 cups boiling water

2 bags mint tea

2 bags chamomile tea

2 bags hibiscus tea

1 cinnamon stick

1 star anise

3 Tbsp agave syrup or coconut palm sugar

1 cup milk (non-dairy or it will curdle; soy, rice or almond)

INSTRUCTIONS

Boil water. Remove from heat; add tea bags and spices and cover for 10 minutes. Strain; add sweetener and milk. Serve right away.

Blood Orange Salad

Serves 4

Perfectly refreshing and acidic enough to help digestion of the animal proteins. Just perfection!

INGREDIENTS

Salad

2 blood oranges, peeled and cut into 8 slices
4 handfuls arugula leaves
1/2 red onion, sliced thin with a mandolin
4 big radishes, sliced thin with a mandolin
12 kalamata olives, pitted and slivered
1/2 cup shaved Parmesan

Vinaigrette

2 Tbsp blood orange juice
1 tsp Dijon mustard
1 Tbsp chopped tarragon leaves
4 Tbsp white or rice vinegar
2 Tbsp olive oil

INSTRUCTIONS

Toss the arugula, onions, olives and radishes into a bowl.

Whisk all vinaigrette ingredients together, until emulsified. Add enough vinaigrette to the salad ingredients to coat. Transfer to serving bowl.

Add blood orange slices on top; baste them with a bit of vinaigrette. Sprinkle the Parmesan shavings go on top.

Grilled Summer Plate

Serves 4

Just delicious and beautiful to the eyes. Proteins and vegetables at their best! Low carb and packed with flavors. Ideally we should have small portions of meats and eat tons of the delicious vegetables.

INGREDIENTS

Meats
    2 chicken breasts (skinless)
    3/4 pound flank steak
    4 small mahi-mahi fillets

Vegetables
    4 1-inch thick eggplant round slices
    8 1-inch thick zucchini slices (cut diagonally, making slices oval)
    8 1-inch thick yellow squash slices (same as above)
    4 1/4-inch red onion slices (keep rings intact)
    1 red pepper, cut into large pieces
    1 yellow peppers, cut into large pieces
    1 large portabella mushroom. cut in 8 triangles

Chimichurri sauce
    1 cup Italian parsley leaves packed tight
    1/2 cup extra virgin olive oil
    2 cloves garlic
    1 tsp kosher salt
    1 tsp red pepper flakes
    3 Tbsp red wine vinegar (or balsamic, for a special touch)

INSTRUCTIONS

Chimichurri sauce: Mix all ingredients in a blender or food processor. Keep at room temp until ready to use.

Meats: Preheat one side of the grill to 450 degrees and the other side at 350 degrees. Thoroughly pat dry meats and fish with paper towels to remove all moisture. Brush the chicken, fish and meat with olive oil. Season with salt and pepper.

Cook the chicken on the hotter side of grill for 2 minutes on each side and transfer to the colder side to finish cooking (chicken is done when really firm to touch about 5 more minutes, depending on thickness of the breast). Cook the fish for 2 minutes on each side and transfer to colder side for a couple more minutes. When cooked through transfer meats to baking sheet. Cook the steaks the same way, making sure to leave them medium or medium rare. Rest meats before slicing.

Vegetables: Brush vegetables with olive oil. Sprinkle with salt and pepper generously. Grill them until beautiful grill marks form, as in the meats.

To serve: Slice the meats on the bias, into half-inch slices. Make sure to slice the steak against the grain (you can see the fiber going in a direction, cut across it). Transfer everything onto a large serving platter, arranging it as beautifully as possible. Brush the meats, fish and vegetables with the chimichurri sauce and serve the extra sauce on the side. Serve hot or at room temperature with a salad.

Minestrone with Grilled Caprese Panini

Serves 6

Heaven on earth. Filling but easy to digest. Delicious and healthy. You can throw a party around it! Please dip that Panini in the soup!

INGREDIENTS

Meatballs for Minestrone

    1/2 pound ground chicken
    1 slice whole-wheat bread, ground in food processor
    1 egg
    1/4 cup Parmesan
    1 tsp Herbes de Provence
    Salt and pepper
    Olive oil for sautéing

Minestrone

    1/2 red onion, chopped
    1 cloves garlic, finely minced
    1 small yellow pepper, diced small
    2 cups chicken stock
    1 small can diced tomatoes
    3/4 cup canned white beans, drained but not rinsed

    12 green beans, cut in small rounds
    1 medium carrot, diced small
    1 broccoli head, just the florets
    1/3 cup basil leaves, chopped
    1 Tbsp fresh oregano leaves

INSTRUCTIONS

Make the meatballs: Mix all the ingredients. Roll into medium-sized meatballs. In a hot Dutch oven, sauté meatballs in olive oil until they are brown on the outside. As they will finish cooking in the broth, they do not need to cook through. Remove the meatballs from the pan.

In the same pan, sauté the onions, garlic and yellow peppers for 3 minutes. Season liberally with salt and pepper. Add the chicken stock, tomatoes and meatballs. Bring to boil, then lower the heat to simmering, cover and cook for 30 minutes.

Add the white beans, green beans and carrots and cook for 10 more minutes. Add the broccoli florets, cook 3 more minutes. Add the basil and oregano. Check for taste. Serve with grilled Caprese panini (opposite page).

Grilled Caprese Panini

Serves 4

INGREDIENTS

4 individual ciabatta breads made with whole-
    wheat flour and no sugar
1 large heirloom tomato, cut into 8 thin slices
8 large fresh basil leaves
1/4 pound fresh mozzarella, sliced into
    1/2 inch slices

INSTRUCTIONS

Preheat oven to 400 degrees.

Cut bread in half horizontally. Brush the inside of each side with olive oil. Cover the bottom slice with fresh mozzarella slices, 2 tomato slices seasoned with salt and pepper. Put the basil leaves on top of the tomato, cover with more mozzarella and top with the bread slice. Brush top slice with olive oil and press the sandwiches down a bit.

Cook the sandwiches in the preheated oven for 10 minutes or use a Panini press. Cut sandwiches diagonally and serve the two halves with a bowl of minestrone soup.

Apple Cinnamon Parfait

Serves 6

Healthy sweet bite at the end of a meal. It can be a great breakfast, too.

INGREDIENTS

Yogurt
    1 1/2 cups Greek yogurt
    2 Tbsp agave syrup
    Zest of 1 orange
    2 Tbsp orange juice
    1 tsp cinnamon

Apples
    2 Granny Smith apples (peeled, cored
        and diced medium)
    2 Fuji apples (same as above)
    2 Tbsp butter
    1 tsp ground fennel seeds
    1/2 cup dried cherries
    1/4 cup apple juice
    2 Tbsp agave syrup

Granola
    3/4 cup whole oats
    1/2 cup chopped walnuts
    2 Tbsp cooking oil
    1/4 cup agave syrup
    1 tsp cinnamon

INSTRUCTIONS

Preheat the oven to 350 degrees.

Prepare the granola: Toss all the ingredients together. Make a 1/2 inch thick layer with the oats on a baking sheet and bake in the oven for 12 to 15 minutes. Leave it to cool and break it into chunks.

Prepare the yogurt mix: Place all the ingredients in a bowl. Refrigerate and reserve until needed.

Prepare the apple compote: In a hot skillet melt the butter. When the butter is about to brown, add the apples and the fennel seeds and sauté for 2 minutes. Add the apple juice, agave syrup and dried cherries and cook until juice is almost completely evaporated and forms a thick sauce in the pan.

Assemble the parfaits: In 4 individual serving bowls, make layers with the yogurt, warm apples and top with granola. Serve immediately.

Breakfast
Lunch
Dinner
Dessert

Thursday

Chef Sergio Galvao

Blueberry and Chocolate Chip Pancakes

Serves 6

Great breakfast for family and kids. So much better than regular pancakes and more delicious.

INGREDIENTS

Batter

1/2 cup whole-wheat flour
1/2 cup ground oatmeal
1/2 Tbsp baking powder
1/3 cup coconut palm sugar
1 egg
1 cup milk (low-fat, almond or rice)
1/4 cup chocolate chips
1/4 cup blueberries (fresh or frozen)

Whipped Cream

3/4 cup heavy cream
1 Tbsp fresh orange zest
1/4 cup agave syrup

Sauce

1 cup blueberries (fresh or frozen)
1/2 cup orange juice

INSTRUCTIONS

Mix first 6 ingredients; let rest for 5 minutes. Add the next 2 ingredients (chips and berries). On a hot griddle sprayed with cooking oil, make pancakes in batches, flipping them just once. Transfer to a warm platter and cover with foil until serving.

For the cream: Whip heavy cream in a mixer until soft peaks form. Add zest and agave syrup and whip for 1 minute more. Save in the fridge until serving.

For blueberry sauce (coulis): Boil blueberries in orange juice for 3 minutes. Puree in a blender until smooth. Serve sauce hot or cold over pancakes with whipped cream.

Smoothie

Serves 2

**A favorite breakfast drink.
When in a hurry, it can become
a breakfast in itself.**

INGREDIENTS

> 2 cups frozen fruits (strawberries, mango, peaches, papaya,
>   berries, pineapple)
> 2 cups orange juice
> 1 cup Greek yogurt
> 1/3 cup agave nectar

INSTRUCTIONS

Blend all ingredients well in a power blender and serve
immediately.

Chicken Curry with Couscous

Serves 4

Complete meal. Easy to digest and filling. A vegetarian version (just skip the chicken) is even lighter and also very nutritious, perfect for a "no-meat" day.

INGREDIENTS

Curry

3 large chicken breasts diced large or
1 lb skinless boneless chicken thighs,
　　cut in 4 pieces each
Salt and pepper
4 Tbsp olive oil
1 red onion diced large (1-inch squares)
1 Tbsp chopped garlic
1 Tbsp freshly grated ginger
2 Tbsp curry powder
1 cup tomato purée or diced tomatoes
1 red pepper, diced large
1 yellow pepper, diced large
2 cups chicken stock
1 cup coconut milk
1 cup baby spinach leaves
1/2 cup chopped cilantro

Couscous

1 cup whole-wheat couscous
1 1/4 cup vegetable stock
1 Tbsp olive oil
1 tsp turmeric
1 tsp salt

INSTRUCTIONS

Season chicken with salt and pepper. In a large Dutch oven heat olive oil until the oil begins to smoke. Sauté chicken until brown and remove it from pan.

In same pan, sauté onions, garlic and ginger until onions are translucent. Add curry powder and sauté 1 minute more. Add tomatoes, peppers, stock, coconut milk and reserved chicken. Season with salt and pepper. Bring to boil, cover and cook for 35 minutes, until chicken is tender and sauce is reduced.

Turn off heat, add spinach leaves and cilantro. Rest for 10 minutes before serving the curry with the couscous.

Prepare the couscous: Boil the stock, turmeric, oil and salt. Add the couscous, turn off the heat and rest for 5 minutes. Fluff the couscous with a fork and serve immediately with the curry.

Week Four / Sergio Galvao

Grilled Swordfish with Mango Salsa over Black Beans and Brown Rice "Risotto"

Serves 4

*Satisfying and flavorful.
It has a Latin vibe to it.
A well-balanced meal.*

INGREDIENTS

Fish
  4 swordfish steaks, 1-inch thick
  2 Tbsp chopped mint
  1 Tbsp garlic powder
  Juice of 1 lemon
  Salt and pepper to taste

Salsa
  1 small firm mango, peeled, pit removed, diced
    small
  1/4 cup red pepper, diced small
  1/4 red onion, chopped fine
  1/4 cup jicama, diced small
  2 Tbsp chopped fresh cilantro
  2 Tbsp red vinegar
  Salt and pepper to taste

Risotto
  1/2 cup brown basmati rice
  3 Tbsp olive oil, divided
  Salt
  1 cup chicken stock (vegetable or beef, if
    preferred)
  1/4 cup chopped onion
  2 cloves garlic, finely minced
  1 Tbsp ground cumin
  1 1/2 cup canned cooked black beans with
    liquid

INSTRUCTIONS

Prepare the salsa: Mix everything together in a bowl and marinate for at least 30 minutes. Salsas don't ask for olive oil but a Tbsp of extra virgin olive oil can be added for richness.

Season the fish steaks with mint, garlic powder, lemon juice, salt and pepper and marinate in the fridge for at least 30 minutes. When it's time, grill them over a hot grill for 3 minutes each side. Flip fish just once. Fish should feel firm, when touched.

Prepare the risotto: Sauté the rice in olive oil in a small pan for 1 minute, just to coat the grains and toast them a bit. Season with salt. Add stock, bring to boil, cover and simmer for 35 minutes, until all the liquid is absorbed.

Meanwhile, sauté onion and garlic in 2 Tbsp olive oil until the onion is translucent. Add cumin, sauté 1 minute more, then add beans and 1/2 cup of the can liquid. Season with salt and pepper. Boil for 10 minutes. Add precooked rice and boil together for 5 minutes. Adjust moisture with black beans liquid, if necessary. "Risotto" is not supposed to be dry or too "soupy" either. Serve the fish over "risotto", topped with salsa.

Sorbet with Fruit Salad and Whole-Wheat Almond Shortbread Cookie

Serves 4

A winner! Just the right amount of cookie accompanied by vitamins, enzymes and mineral packed fruits that just burst with flavor and deliciousness. It doesn't get healthier than that!

INGREDIENTS

Sorbet

3 cups mixed frozen fruits
(strawberries, peaches, apricots, pineapple)
1 cup orange juice
1/3 cup agave syrup

Fruit salad

3 cups diced fresh ripe fruits
(mango, kiwi, strawberry, pears, apples form great combination)
2 Tbsp chopped fresh mint
1/4 cup orange juice
1 Tbsp agave syrup
Pinch of cinnamon

Cookie

3/4 cup whole-wheat flour
1/2 cup almond meal (ground raw almonds)
1/2 cup coconut palm sugar
1/2 cup butter, room temperature
1 egg
1 tsp cinnamon

INSTRUCTIONS

Prepare the sorbet: Blend all ingredients together in a power blender. Freeze until serving.

Prepare the fruit salad: Toss it all together and let sit for at least 30 minutes.

For the cookies: Preheat the oven to 375 degrees. Mix all ingredients well. Add a bit of cold water if necessary to make the dough come together. Refrigerate the dough until chilled. Roll dough 1/2-inch thick over a lightly floured cold surface. Use a cookie cutter or a knife to shape the cookies. Bake for 15 minutes on parchment paper on a baking sheet.

Serve a scoop of sorbet with fruit salad and garnish with a cookie and mint leaves.

Week Four / Sergio Galvao

Breakfast
Lunch
Dinner
Dessert

Friday

Chef Sergio Galvao

Milkshake

Serves 2

Appeals to our inner child and very good for you too.

INGREDIENTS

2 cups frozen fruits
3 cups milk (low-fat if preferred)
1/4 cup agave syrup

INSTRUCTIONS

Blend all ingredients well in power blender and serve right away.

Waffle with Greek Yogurt and Fruits

Serves 6

Another Sunday morning favorite that works any day of the week. Light in protein and rich in everything else.

INGREDIENTS

Batter
> 3/4 cup whole-wheat flour
>
> 1/4 cup ground walnuts
>
> 1 tsp baking powder
>
> 1 tsp salt
>
> 2 Tbsp coconut palm sugar
>
> 2 eggs
>
> 1 cup buttermilk
>
> 1/4 cup unsalted butter, melted
>
> Cooking spray for waffle maker

Yogurt
> 1 cup Greek yogurt
>
> 1/3 cup coconut palm sugar
>
> 2 Tbsp orange zest
>
> 1 tsp cinnamon

Berries
> 1 1/2 cup mixed berries (sliced strawberries, blueberries, blackberries and raspberries)
>
> 4 Tbsp agave nectar
>
> 1/4 cup orange juice

INSTRUCTIONS

Prepare the berries: Mix and macerate the berries for at least 30 minutes (so they create a sauce of their own).

For the waffles: Preheat the oven to 200 degrees. Mix the dry ingredients in a large bowl. Mix the wet ingredients in a separate bowl. Pour the wet ingredients over the dry ingredients and mix well, but don't over-mix. Let the batter rest for 10 minutes before starting to make the waffles in a preheated waffle maker, sprayed with cooking spray. Transfer the waffles to a baking sheet and cover with foil to keep warm in the oven until serving time.

Prepare the yogurt: Mix all ingredients together.

To serve: Put a scoop of yogurt over the hot waffle and serve the berries alongside.

Week Four / Sergio Galvao

Grilled Romaine Salad

Week Four / Sergio Galvao

Serves 2

An easy way to make a sophisticated meal. Delicious by itself or with a grilled piece of fish or chicken by its side.

INGREDIENTS

> 2 heads of romaine lettuce (just the inner
> 　　leaves, cut in half lengthwise)
> 1 cup cherry tomatoes, halved
> 1/2 cup blue cheese crumbles
> 1/3 cup pine nuts, toasted

Dressing
> 3/4 cup buttermilk
> 1/4 cup Greek yogurt
> 1/4 cup chopped herbs (parsley, thyme, mint,
> 　　tarragon)
> 3 Tbsp olive oil
> 1 lemon, juiced

INSTRUCTIONS

Mix together all the ingredients for the dressing. Season with salt and pepper.

For the salad: Brush the romaine halves with olive oil and grill them on a very hot grill. Get nice grill marks on them but don't grill them for too long, so they're still crispy inside.

Put each half on a plate, pour some ranch dressing over them. Add tomatoes, blue cheese crumbles and pine nuts and serve immediately.

Shepherd's Pie

Serves 6

Comfort food that everybody loves! Proteins, carbs and healthy vegetables all-in-one. It is rich and filling and lighter than the traditional version.

INGREDIENTS

- 3/4 lb ground beef
- 1/2 onion, chopped
- 2 cloves garlic, finely minced
- 1 cup diced or crushed tomatoes
- 3/4 cup beef, vegetable or even chicken stock
- 2 Tbsp chopped thyme or rosemary
- 1/2 cup red pepper, diced small
- 1/2 cup frozen peas
- 1 lb sweet potatoes
- 1/2 cup heavy cream
- 2 Tbsp butter
- 1/3 cup grated Parmesan cheese
- 1 egg mixed with 2 Tbs milk (egg wash)

INSTRUCTIONS

Preheat the oven to 400 degrees.

In a medium saucepan, sauté the onion and garlic in olive oil. Add meat, sauté, breaking the meat lumps until the meat begins to brown and any juices have evaporated. Add the peppers and sauté for 2 minutes. Add the tomatoes, stock and chopped herbs. Cover with a fitting lid and cook for 20 minutes.

Remove the lid and, over medium heat, allow the excess liquid to evaporate and the sauce to thicken. Season with salt and pepper to taste. Take the meat off the heat and add frozen peas.

Meanwhile bake the sweet potatoes for 30 minutes, or until a paring knife easily pierces the potato skin and flesh. Rest the potatoes for a few minutes, but, while still warm, cut them open, scoop the flesh from the skin and put in a mixing bowl. Add the butter, cream, Parmesan and season with salt and pepper to taste. Mix well.

Reduce the oven temperature to 375 degrees. In individual 10-oz ramekins, put a thin layer of sweet potato purée in the bottom of the ramekin. Cover with 1/4 of the meat sauce and cover with another layer of sweet potato purée. Brush with the egg wash. Transfer the ramekins to a baking sheet and bake until brown on the top and bubbly. Serve with the salad.

Asparagus Cream Soup with Chicken Sandwich

Serves 4

An elegant and healthy way to entertain and nourish our friends.

INGREDIENTS

Asparagus Soup

     1 bunch asparagus, stems and tips

     1/2 large onion, chopped

     3 cloves garlic, finely minced

     1 Tbsp olive oil

     3 cups chicken stock

     1 cup sweet potato puree (roasted and mashed sweet potato)

     1/2 cup heavy cream

     1 Tbsp rice vinegar

Chicken Sandwich

     2 medium-sized boneless and skinless chicken breasts, butterflied into 4 fillets

     1 cup baby spinach leaves

     8 thick slices smoked provolone cheese

     8 slices whole-wheat bread

     1 large tomato cut into 8 slices

     1/4 cup Dijon mustard

     1/4 cup mayonnaise

INSTRUCTIONS

Make the soup: Heat a large saucepan over high heat. Sauté the onion and garlic in olive oil. Add the chicken stock and bring to boil. Add the asparagus tips and cook, one minute at most or until just tender. Scoop out of the boiling liquid and reserve for garnish.

Add the asparagus stems to the boiling stock and cook until tender. Transfer to a power blender and blend well until smooth. Pass the puréed asparagus through a medium sieve, pressing well to extract the pulp of the asparagus through the sieve with a rubber spatula, leaving just the tough fiber behind.

Place the strained asparagus purée back into the saucepan. Add the mashed potato purée, cream and bring to boil. The soup should be velvety and thick but still consistent with soup. Check seasoning, adding salt and pepper if needed. Add the vinegar and mix well.

Prepare the sandwiches: Season the chicken fillets with salt and pepper. Sauté them in very hot skillet, with olive oil. Flip them just once, when they become white at the edge. Transfer them to a plate.

Put four slices of bread side by side and brush them with a mix of Dijon mustard and mayonnaise. Put one slice of cheese on each bread. Cover with baby spinach leaves and put one chicken fillet over it. Cover with another cheese slice and another bread slice brushed with Dijon mustard and mayonnaise mixture.

Grill all four sandwiches in a hot skillet with olive oil. Cut them diagonally into two triangles each. Serve immediately with the hot soup, garnished with the reserved asparagus tips.

Fruit Crumble

Serves 4

Served bubbly from the oven with a scoop of low fat, sugar-free ice-cream, you cannot go wrong. Healthy and amazing!

INGREDIENTS

1 apple, peeled, cored and diced
1 pear, peeled, cored and diced
3/4 cup raspberries (fresh or frozen)
3/4 cup blueberries (fresh or frozen)
2 Tbsp lemon juice
1 Tbsp lemon zest
1 tsp cinnamon (or pumpkin pie seasoning)
1 1/2 Tbsp whole-wheat flour
1/3 cup agave syrup or coconut palm sugar

Crumble top

1 cup oatmeal
1/2 cup ground (or finely chopped) walnuts
2 Tbsp whole-wheat flour

INSTRUCTIONS

Preheat oven to 400 degrees. Toss the ingredients of the crumble together in a mixing bowl. If using frozen berries, do not thaw them.

In a large bowl, mix all the ingredients of the crumble together, melting the butter with the heat of your hands, to create a coarse crumble mix.

In 4 individual 10-oz ramekins, pour the fruit in the bottom and top it with the crumble. Place the ramekins on a baking sheet and bake them in the preheated oven for 35 to 40 minutes, until the top is golden and bubbly and syrup oozes through the top crust.

Serve hot as it is or with a scoop of no-sugar-added vanilla ice cream.

Breakfast
Lunch
Dinner
Dessert

Saturday

Chef Sergio Galvao

Mango Kefir

Serves 2

You feel good after just one sip of it. Your whole body will thank you.

INGREDIENTS

2 cups mango slices, puréed (thawed if frozen)
1 1/2 cup plain Greek yogurt
1 cup orange juice
1/3 cup agave syrup

INSTRUCTIONS

Blend all ingredients well and serve immediately.

Spinach Crêpe

Serves 4

As chic and delicious as it gets. You can actually use anything for a filling and make it sweet or savory.

INGREDIENTS

Batter
> 1 1/2 cup milk
> 3/4 cup whole-wheat flour
> 1 egg
> 1 tsp baking powder
> Salt and pepper to taste

Filling
> 4 cups baby spinach leaves
> 1 clove garlic, minced
> 1 cup ricotta cheese, drained in strainer,
>   over cheese cloth or kitchen towel
> 1/2 cup grated Parmesan cheese

Béchamel
> 1 1/2 cup milk
> 2 Tbsp butter
> 3 Tbsp whole-wheat flour
> 1/2 tsp ground nutmeg
> Salt and pepper to taste

INSTRUCTIONS

Prepare the batter: Mix everything well. Let the batter rest for 10 minutes. Make crêpes in a hot medium size skillet brushed with butter or sprayed with cooking oil. Use 1/4 cup batter for each crêpe. Flip them just once. Pile them up on a plate as you make them.

For the filling: Sauté spinach in olive oil and garlic, until the spinach starts to wilt. Drain any excess liquid. Mix spinach with ricotta and Parmesan. Season with salt and pepper.

For the béchamel: Melt the butter in saucepan and add the flour. Sauté the flour for one minute. Add the cold milk and mix well with a whisk. Season with nutmeg, salt and pepper. Bring to a boil and cook until it covers the back of a spoon.

Assemble the crêpes: Put a bit of spinach ricotta mix in the center of each crêpe. Roll them like cigars and put them side-by-side in a baking dish. Pour béchamel over them and sprinkle some Parmesan cheese. Broil until the crêpes start browning on top. Serve right away.

Meatloaf Roulade with Mashed Cauliflower and Sautéed Vegetables

Serves 4

Again, food for the whole family. Everybody will love it and they'll never think of it as a "healthy food". Mashed cauliflower is as delicious as mashed potatoes and most people will not notice the difference.

INGREDIENTS

Meatloaf

3/4 lb ground turkey (dark meat is better)

1 cup fresh breadcrumbs (3 or 4 slices whole-wheat bread in food processor)

1 egg

1/2 cup grated Parmesan cheese

1/3 cup chopped parsley

1 Tbsp herbs de Provence

2 Tbsp Worcestershire sauce (or soy sauce, if preferred)

Filling

3/4 cup chopped sundried tomatoes

1 cup spinach leaves

3/4 cup grated mozzarella cheese

Gravy

4 cups turkey or chicken stock, boiled until reduced to 2 cups

2 Tbsp whole-wheat flour

2 Tbsp butter

1 bay leaf

Mashed Cauliflower

1 large head cauliflower

1 Tbsp butter

1/4 cup sour cream

1/4 cup Parmesan

Vegetables

1 large zucchini, cut in 4 lengthwise, seeded and cut into sticks on the diagonal

1 large red pepper, cut into strips

2 cups mushrooms, sliced

1 clove garlic

Juice of 1 lemon

INSTRUCTIONS

Preheat the oven to 400 degrees.

Prepare the meatloaf: Mix all the ingredients for the meatloaf. Season with salt and pepper. Spread over a surface covered in plastic film, forming a rectangle 3/4 inch thick.

Spread the filling ingredients over the meat, leaving 2 inches free in every corner. With the help of the plastic wrap, roll the meat into a roulade, pressing well to keep everything tight. You can now put the roulade in a loaf pan or bake it on a baking sheet.

Bake it in the preheated oven for 40 minutes (internal temperature 165 degrees with meat thermometer). Rest the meatloaf before slicing.

Make the cauliflower: Place cauliflower in a small pan. Put 1/2-inch water in the bottom of pan. Cover, bring to boil and move lid to the side, so steam can escape. Simmer until cauliflower is very tender, and almost no liquid is left. Drain cauliflower. Pat dry if necessary.

In a food processor, purée cauliflower well. Transfer purée to a pan. Add butter, cream and cheese. Season with salt and pepper and cook it until it reaches the right consistency. It should look just like regular mashed potatoes.

Sauté the vegetables: Sauté garlic with olive oil in a hot skillet. Add vegetables and sauté for 3 minutes. Season with salt and pepper. Add lemon juice and keep sautéing for 1 minute more. Veggies are ready when browned, but still crispy and not mushy.

Prepare the gravy: Melt butter in a saucepan. Add flour, stir for 1 minute. Pour the cold reduced stock slowly, whisking to avoid lumps. Add the bay leaf and bring it to boil. Cook until slightly thickened. Remove bay leaf from the gravy. Serve a slice of the meatloaf on the top of the cauliflower puree and sautéed vegetables. Drizzle everything with the gravy.

Strawberry Salad

Serves 4

Perfect side for any dish. Light and refreshing, it helps the digestion.

INGREDIENTS

Salad

    1 cup strawberries, quartered

    3 cups baby spinach leaves

    1/2 cup red onions, finely sliced with mandoline

    1/2 cup toasted almonds (slivered or shaved)

    Feta cheese, crumbled (optional)

Vinaigrette

    1 Tbsp Dijon mustard

    1/4 cup balsamic vinegar

    1/4 cup olive oil

    Salt and pepper to taste

INSTRUCTIONS

Whisk ingredients for vinaigrette together until emulsified.

Toss spinach, strawberries, onions and almonds with just enough vinaigrette to coat it. Sprinkle some crumbled feta cheese on top for extra richness or serve as is.

Chicken Cordon Bleu and Brown Rice Asparagus Risotto

Serves 4

Even more delicious than the deep-fried version, this is an elegant dinner that you can serve to anyone. After trying a risotto made with brown rice, you may never want to use high-glycemic Arborio rice again.

INGREDIENTS

Chicken
4 small chicken breast fillets
4 slices smoked turkey
4 slices mozzarella cheese
4 Tbsp whole-wheat flour
1 egg mixed with 1 Tbsp water (egg-wash)
8 Tbsp whole-wheat bread crumbs
1 Tbsp garlic powder
1 tsp Herbes de Provence
Salt and pepper

Week Four / Sergio Galvao

Risotto

> *3/4 cup short grain brown rice*
> *1 1/2 cup chicken stock*
> *2 cups asparagus, cut small*
> *1/2 cup chicken stock*
> *1 clove garlic*
> *1 Tbsp butter*
> *1/4 cup heavy cream*
> *1/4 cup grated Parmesan cheese*
> *Salt and pepper*

INSTRUCTIONS

Prep the rice: Precook brown rice in 1 1/2 cup chicken stock for 35 minutes. Pour rice over baking sheet and spread it to cool fast. Set aside.

Preheat oven to 400 degrees.

Prepare the chicken: With a knife, make a large pocket in each chicken breast, taking care not to completely cut through. Insert one slice of turkey and one slice of cheese in the pocket.

Season chicken fillets with salt, pepper, Herbes de Provence and garlic powder. Sprinkle fillets with whole-wheat flour and remove excess by gently tapping them. Coat fillets with egg-wash and press breadcrumbs into the surface so that it adheres well. Sauté the fillets in hot olive oil in oven proof skillet and when brown on both sides, transfer the skillet to the preheated oven for 10 minutes.

Finish the risotto: In a large skillet, sauté garlic in butter for a minute. Add asparagus and cook for 1 more minute. Season with salt and pepper. Add 1/2 cup chicken stock, reserved rice and heavy cream. Cook the risotto for 5 minutes, until excess liquid is absorbed and asparagus is tender. Add the Parmesan cheese.

Remove chicken from the oven and let rest before serving. Plate a portion of risotto on each plate. Serve immediately topped with the chicken. Enjoy!

No-Bake Cheesecake with Raspberry Coulis

Serves 4

Clients love it. Easier to make than the baked version, it also feels lighter. Delicious!

INGREDIENTS

Cheesecake

> 3/4 cup heavy cream, cold
>
> 8 oz cream cheese, room temperature
>
> 1/3 cup agave syrup
>
> 1 Tbsp non-alcohol vanilla
>
> 1 Tbsp orange zest
>
> 1 envelope gelatin (dissolved in 6 Tbsp water and microwaved until translucent; follow package instructions)

Crust

> 2/3 cup ground walnuts
>
> 3 Tbsp melted butter
>
> 2 Tbsp coconut palm sugar

Raspberry Coulis

> 1 cup raspberries (fresh or frozen)
>
> 2 Tbsp apple or orange juice
>
> 2 Tbsp agave syrup

INSTRUCTIONS

Prepare the cheesecake: Lightly spray four 7-oz ramekins with cooking oil and cover the bottom with foil cut to the exact size of the bottom of the ramekins.

Whip the heavy cream until soft peaks form. Gently fold the soft cream cheese into whipped cream. Add the agave syrup, vanilla, zest and dissolved gelatin and mix well. Split the mixture into the ramekins and place in the refrigerator to set.

For the crust: Mix the ingredients well and put on the top of cream cheese mix in the ramekins, after cream cheese mix is beginning to set. Press gently. Put back in the refrigerator to set.

For the raspberry coulis: Boil all ingredients for 5 minutes. Blend well and strain through a fine sieve.

Unmold cheesecakes onto a dessert plates. Use a paring knife to help release them from ramekins, if necessary. Crust will now be on the bottom. Drizzle coulis on the top of cheesecakes and garnish with fresh raspberries and mint leaves.

Breakfast
Lunch
Dinner
Dessert

Sunday

Chef Sergio Galvao

Chocolate Milkshake

Serves 4

Serotonin booster that just makes you feel happy right away!

INGREDIENTS

4 scoops chocolate ice cream (recipe follows)
3 cups milk
2 Tbsp coconut palm sugar

INSTRUCTIONS

Blend all ingredients well and serve right away.

Chocolate Ice Cream (to be made ahead)

INGREDIENTS

1 cup oatmeal
3 cups milk
1/3 cup coconut palm sugar
1 Tbsp non-alcohol vanilla extract
1 cup unsweetened cocoa powder

INSTRUCTIONS

Bring oatmeal and milk to boil in a heavy saucepan. Cook for 5 minutes. Cool the mixture for 10 minutes and blend it in a power blender, until smooth. If you like a little texture, don't blend it too much.

While still warm, transfer to a bowl, add coconut palm sugar, vanilla and chocolate, mixing well. After the mixture has cooled down, freeze in an ice cream maker or freeze in a container, mixing every 30 minutes, until completely set and smooth.

Pita Breakfast Pizza

Serves 4

Fun and good for you. Easy to make, it packs a lot of nutrition and flavor. Children love it as well.

INGREDIENTS

4 small whole-wheat pita breads
3/4 cup tomato sauce
6 eggs, beaten with 3 Tbsp milk
1/2 lb ground turkey
1/2 cup red onion, sliced thin in mandolin
1/3 cup Kalamata olives, chopped
1/2 cup feta cheese, crumbled

INSTRUCTIONS

Preheat oven to 400 degrees.

Season ground turkey with salt, pepper and red pepper flakes. Shape it like a burger and sauté in a hot skillet.

When you flip to brown the other side, break it with a spatula into big chunks. Cook through, until golden.

In a separate skillet, scramble eggs, cook them almost to the end, slightly under cooked.

Put pita breads side by side on a baking sheet. Cover each one with tomato sauce, turkey, scrambled eggs, onions, olives and feta cheese. Bake for 10 minutes. Serve hot.

Caprese Kebabs

Serves 4

A little touch of fun for the meal. It complements a meal perfectly.

INGREDIENTS

8 cherry tomatoes, halved
8 bocconcini cheese balls
    (same size as tomatoes), halved
8 basil leaves, halved
4 wooden skewers, large
2 Tbsp balsamic
2 Tbsp olive oil
1 tsp Dijon mustard

INSTRUCTIONS

Put half a tomato and half a cheese ball together and skewer it. Put a basil leaf half next to it and repeat 4 times. Make 4 skewers like this.

Mix vinaigrette ingredients together and serve in a small container next to the skewer on the plate.

Pesto-Roasted Red Snapper with Lemon Parmesan Fettuccine

Serves 4

Easy to make, fast and delicious lunch.

INGREDIENTS

Fish

    4 8-oz red snapper fillets
    1/2 cup basil leaves
    1/4 cup grated Parmesan cheese
    2 garlic cloves
    1/4 cup toasted pine nuts
    1/4 cup olive oil
    1/4 cup whole-wheat panko breadcrumbs
    Salt and pepper to taste

Lemon Parmesan Fettuccine

    3/4 pound whole-wheat fettuccine
    1/4 cup lemon juice
    1 Tbsp lemon zest
    1/4 cup grated Parmesan cheese
    1/4 cup olive oil
    Salt and pepper to taste

INSTRUCTIONS

Preheat oven to 400 degrees.

In a food processor, mix basil, Parmesan, garlic, pine nuts, olive oil, and salt and pepper until you get a nice paste. In a bowl, mix panko crumbs into pesto. Season fish with salt and pepper and spread a thick layer of the pesto with panko on the top of fish.

Place fillets on a baking sheet brushed with oil and bake for 15 minutes, until the fish feels firm when touched with finger and crust is lightly brown.

Cook pasta al dente. In a bowl, mix lemon juice, zest, Parmesan and olive oil. Toss hot pasta in this sauce, salt and pepper to taste and serve topped by the fish fillet.

Week Four / Sergio Galvao

Beef Meatballs with Traditional Tomato Sauce and Mashed Butternut Squash

Serves 4

Familiar, comforting and delicious. The squash is another replacement for mashed potatoes that is even lighter.

INGREDIENTS

Meatballs

    3/4 lb ground beef

    3/4 cup fresh whole-wheat bread crumbs

    1 egg

    1/2 cup Parmesan

    1/3 cup chopped parsley

    1 Tbsp Herbes de Provence

    2 Tbsp soy sauce

Tomato Sauce

    1/2 onion, chopped

    2 cloves garlic, minced

    1 fennel bulb, chopped

    1 tsp fennel seeds, ground

    2 cups diced tomatoes

    1 cup beef, vegetable or even chicken stock

    1 cup sweet peas, frozen

    1/4 cup chopped parsley

Squash

    1 medium butternut squash

    1 tsp garlic powder

    1/2 tsp cinnamon

    2 Tbsp butter, cold

    1/4 cup grated Parmesan

    Salt and pepper to taste

INSTRUCTIONS

Preheat oven to 400 degrees.

Start butternut squash: Put squash whole on a baking sheet and roast for 30 to 40 minutes, until a paring knife easily pierces skin and flesh of the squash. Keep the oven on for the meatballs.

Start meatballs: Mix all the meatball ingredients until combined, don't overmix. With an ice cream scoop, shape meatballs and put them on a greased baking sheet. Bake them in the oven for 15 minutes. They should be firm to the touch and golden. Pay attention not to overcook them.

Finish the squash: After the squash cools down enough to handle, cut in half, scoop seeds out and remove flesh from skin. Add all other ingredients to pulp and mix well. Set aside,

For the tomato sauce: In a saucepan, sauté onion, garlic, fennel bulb and seeds in olive oil. Add tomatoes and stock and cook for 30 minutes.

If necessary, reduce a bit more to your preferred consistency. Add peas and parsley, roasted meatballs and boil for 1 minute more. Serve immediately over the mashed squash. If you like, shave some fresh Parmesan on top.

Brazilian Walnut Cake With Whipped Cream and Coconut Sauce

Serves 6

Flourless, sugar-free and with just enough richness to make it decadent. Nice way to celebrate somebody's birthday!

INGREDIENTS

Cake
- 4 eggs, whites and yolks separated
- 1/3 pound ground walnuts
- 1/3 cup coconut palm sugar
- 1 Tbsp ground oatmeal

Coconut sauce
- 1 can coconut milk
- 1/4 cup agave syrup
- 1/4 cup oatmeal flour (ground in food processor until very fine)
- 2 tsp turmeric
- 1 tsp butter

Whipped cream
- 1/2 cup whipping cream, cold
- 1 tsp non-alcohol vanilla extract
- 2 Tbsp agave syrup

INSTRUCTIONS

Preheat the oven to 350 degrees.

Prepare cake: Spray 4 10-oz ramekins with cooking spray and line the bottom of each ramekin with a circle of foil. Beat the egg whites until stiff. Add the egg yolks, walnuts, coconut palm sugar and oatmeal gently, stirring just to combine everything. Fill the prepared ramekins and bake for 15 minutes or until a toothpick comes out clean. Cool the cakes for 5 minutes and unmold them while still a bit warm. After they have cooled down, cut them in two layers with a serrated knife.

Coconut sauce: Cook all the ingredients together until thickened. Reserve.

Make whipped cream: Beat the cream in the bowl of a mixer until soft peaks form. Add vanilla and agave syrup. Leave in the refrigerator until time to serve.

To serve: Cover the bottom half of cake with coconut sauce. Place the top layer of the cake over the coconut sauce and cover it with whipped cream. Drizzle coconut sauce over the cake in a nice pattern and serve.

SHOPPING LISTS FOR
THE MALIBU BEACH RECOVERY DIET

WHOLE FOODS MARKETS

Whole-wheat pastas

Whole grains: quinoa, wheat berries, farro, kasha, barley, spelt, buckwheat, brown rice

Organic meats: beef, lamb, veal, bison – raised without antibiotics or hormones and grass fed preferably

Organic poultry: chicken, duck, turkey, cornish game hens

Sustainable fish: all kinds, not farm raised – salmon is rich in antioxidants

Organic fruits: all fruits except melons (watermelons, Tuscan, honeydew), bananas and grapes

Organic vegetables: kale, collard greens, lettuce, zucchini, eggplant, cauliflower (the richer in color, the better)

Root vegetables: carrots, beets

Breads made entirely with whole-wheat flour, salt and yeast

Cold cuts (be careful as they often contain sugar in the brine or the glaze)

Prepared foods made without sugar, corn by-products or white flour – read labels carefully

TRADER JOE'S

Whole-wheat couscous

Half-and-half

Unsalted butter: Kerry Gold grass fed

Oils: olive, sesame and coconut

Vinegars

Whole-wheat pastas or Dreamfields brand pasta

Frozen fruits

Frozen vegetables

Roasted red peppers

Tapenades and other spreads (read ingredients)

Salsas and hummus

Eggs (omega 3)

Cheeses (Brie, Parmesan, Madrigal, Jarlsberg, goat cheese)

Fage Greek yogurt 0 percent and 2%

Meats (no pork)

Organic chicken breasts

Fish (fresh and frozen)

Shrimp

Vegetables and fruits (according to seasons)

Herbs

Himalayan pink salt

Lemons and limes

Breads (Ezekiel, Pain Pascal, whole-wheat pita and mini pitas) Artisan breads without honey or sugar

Whole grain baguette for crostini

Nuts (make your own combinations)

SHOPPING LIST BY CATEGORY

Breads

Breads and English muffins with lots of grains

Pumpernickel bread

Sourdough (whole grain, rye or whole wheat)

Breakfast Cereals

Whole bran cereals (not bran flakes)

Oatmeal made from whole grain traditional rolled oats or steel-cut oats (not instant or quick-cooking oats)

Natural granola with no or few cereal flakes and no sugar or honey

Grains for boiling (to be served with meals or added to soups or salads)

Barley: pearled or cracked

Basmati rice

Wild rice

Quinoa

Whole buckwheat kernels (bulgur)

Whole rye kernels

Pasta and Noodles

All types of durum wheat pasta, fresh or dried, with small extrusions (spaghetti, angel hair, etc.)

Whole-wheat pasta

Soba noodles

Cookies

Stoneground flour and dried fruit cookies

Oatmeal cookies

Fruit

Fresh: apples, pears, oranges, mandarins, tangerines, grapefruit, plums, apricots, nectarines, peaches, berries, kiwi fruit, mangoes, avocado

Dried: apple, apricot, pear, peach, prunes, golden raisins, mango

Fruit juices (pure, unsweetened, no added sugar): apple, grapefruit, orange, pineapple, tomato, cranberry

Vegetables – Fresh, canned and frozen

Sweet potatoes, yams

Onions, garlic, shallots, leeks, herbs, arugula, ginger, chilies, tomatoes, lettuce, celery, cucumber, cabbage, mushrooms, Brussels sprouts, broccoli, cauliflower, pepper, spinach, green beans, kale, bean sprouts, alfalfa, zucchini, eggplant, artichoke, endive, chard, bok choy, okra, asparagus

Legumes

All types of raw or dry roasted nuts and seeds: almonds, flax seed, pecans, sunflower seeds, walnuts

All types of legumes, dried, canned, vacuum packed: lentils, chickpeas, soy beans, kidney beans, cannellini

Hummus

Tofu

Tempeh

Canned baked beans

Dairy Products

Cow's milk: full fat, reduced fat and nonfat

Soymilk, calcium enriched

Kefir

Yogurt: Greek 0% and 2% with no sugar added

Ice cream: sugar free

Pudding: made from instant mix with milk – sugar free

All types of cheese: Cheddar, feta, mozzarella, Parmesan, ricotta

Beverages

Bottled water

Teas: non-caffeinated

Juices that are low on the glycemic index: apple juice, carrot juice, orange juice

Sweeteners and Other Pantry Staples

Splenda / Stevia

Fruit spreads and jam with no added sugar

Yeast extract spreads

Mayonnaise and salad dressings (no sugar added)

Vinegar, mustard, chili sauce

Dried herbs and spices, capers, fresh herb mixes

Diet gelatin desserts

Reduced sodium tamari sauce

Extra virgin olive oil, coconut oil

Olive oil spray, coconut oil spray

Lime and lemon juices

Fleur de sel

Himalayan pink salt

Truffle salt

Meat, Poultry, Fish and Seafood – fresh, frozen and canned

Lean cuts of meat and lower-fat premium ground meats

Poultry: fresh or frozen and eaten without the skin

Eggs: omega 3

Fish: fresh, frozen or canned in spring water

Seafood: fresh or frozen

Soups

Minestrone

Lentil

Tomato

Clear beef, chicken or vegetable broths

MENU PLANS BY CHEF
Chef Yannick Marchand

Chef Licia Jaccard

Chef Johnnie Handal

Chef Sergio Galvao

INDEX

Acknowledgements

My dear husband, Oleg Vidov, for his constant love, patience and encouragement.

Kenneth Blum, PhD for his wealth of knowledge and steadfast support.

Mark Gold, MD for his insight.

Licia Jaccard, Yannick Marchand, Sergio Galvao and Johnnie Handal for taking the time to memorialize their best meals as written recipes.

Executive Chef Cyril Landrat, who tested many of the recipes.

Leonid Katsnelson, our very talented graphic artist, who had the vision required to bring our project to fruition.

Hanan Sher, my former editor at the Jerusalem Post, for making us sound good. Larry Zimberg, for his wordsmithing talents. Sarah Minot Gold for her organizational skills.

Pat Olsen, who writes for our blog and helped the chefs craft their biographies.

Licia Jaccard for compiling "How the Malibu Beach Recovery Diet Works" and accompanying lists.

Art director Yelena Burnett and photographer Tom Moy.

Victor Panov, PJ Letofsky and Aleksandr Rudenskiy for photographing the chefs and their food.

Angela Goncalves, who always helps me make things happen, and her right hand, Liz Hernandez.

My stepson, Sergei Vidov, for encouraging me.

Our friends Jeffrey Miles and Kim Crowe, Russ and Kathy Jura, Joel and Charlotte Parker.

Dorothea Shackleton for sourcing the best chef jackets. Seth Isler and Susan Sullivan for producing our first cookbook video and of course China Cantner Isler.

Our friends at Harborcove and Insight Healthcare — we love you.

Nigel Yorwerth and Patricia Spadaro, my publishing coaches, for their expert help and guidance.

All of the alumni and their families who kept asking, "Where is my cookbook?"

Photo by Annie Wells. Copyright *Los Angeles Times*. Reprinted with permission.

Joan Borsten is the co-founder with her husband, Oleg Vidov, of the Malibu Beach Recovery Center. She served as CEO until 2014 and expanded operations to include a women's only facility in West Los Angeles. Both treatment centers and an affiliated Intensive Outpatient Program have been acquired by RiverMend Health and Joan now works with them as senior advisor. She wrote this cookbook with four of the Malibu Beach Recovery Center chefs as part of her commitment to help her alumni as well as addicts around the world maintain long-term sobriety.

Joan graduated from the University of California at Berkeley and did her graduate work at University of Southern California.

She served as a Peace Corps volunteer in rural Panama before moving to Israel, where she became a staff reporter for *The Jerusalem Post* and then a regular contributor to the *Los Angeles Times*. She traveled worldwide on assignment, interviewing Egyptian First Lady Jehan Sadat, Tunisian First Lady Wasilla Bourguiba and film industry luminaries such as Federico Fellini, Ingrid Bergman, Jack Lemmon, George C. Scott, Raul Julia, Tony Curtis, Bruce Beresford, Roman Polanski and Walter Matthau. Joan began a career in the film industry as executive of two companies that won Best Foreign Film Oscars and went on to found the film production and distribution company Films by Jove Inc. with her husband.